Schedule Quantitative Risk Analysis
(Traditional Method)

RUFRAN C. FRAGO

P. Eng., PMP®, CCP, PMI-RMP®

Schedule Quantitative Risk Analysis

(Traditional Method)

Authored and Self-published by: Rufran C. Frago

For general information on our other products and services, please contact the Author/Publisher using e-mail address consultant@pmsolutionpro.com

For information about licensing the book brand or for related consulting, products, training and services, contact consultant@pmsolutionpro.com

PM Solution Pro
(Risk-based Management and Services Inc.)
PO Box 24083, Calgary, Alberta
Canada   T2Y 0J9

KDP ISBN : 9781794241688

ISBN ISBN: 978-0-9947608-3-8 (Canada)

Dedication

Thank You God for all Your blessings, for without You, nothing is possible.

My deepest love and appreciation to Ann, my better half for helping me appreciate patience and perseverance, for inspiring me to develop, to create, and to nurture new ideas. This book would not come to fruition without her precious support.

To my family, especially my lovely grandkids Eva, Mia, and Grace from Him who created all, for moving me to write.

To real friends, mentors, and colleagues in the profession, who contributed one way or another in completing this book, my sincere appreciation!

Rufran C. Frago

P. Eng., PMP®, CCP, PMI-RMP®, Author

Calgary, Alberta, Canada

Contents

Dedication i

Contents iii

List of Figures vii

Preface xi

Icons in this Book xv

Acknowledgments xvii

1. Introduction 1

2. Definitions 5

3. SQRA 7

4. Visualizing Risk 11

5. Visualizing Impact 13

6. Visualizing Probability 17

7. Risk Simulation 19

8. Tools and Techniques 23

9. SQRA Benefits 27

10. Contingency 29

11. Duration Range 31

12. Three-Point Estimate 37

13. Data Quality 39

14. Schedule Validation 43

15. Calendars 45

16. Baseline Schedule 51

17. Schedule Filter 53

18. Static Path 55

19. Integrated Analysis 57

20. Schedule Risk Model 59

    20-1   Very High-Level Summary (VHLS) 59

    20-2   Medium Level Summary 60

    20-3   Fit for Purpose Model 61

    20-4   Summary Model 65

21. VHLS Proponents 67

22. Stop using VHLS? 69

23. Contracts & Schedules 73

24. Optimum Size 77

25. Detailed Schedule 79

26. ICSQRA 81

27. Political Dates 83

28.   Which model to use? 87

29.   SQRA Preparation 91

30.   Engagement Process 99

31.   Required Participants 105

32.   Modeling Philosophy 107

33.   Guide to Ranging.......................................111

34.   Avoid Double-dipping 115

35.   Common issues.. 117

36.   Import Issues.. 119

37.   Review, Fix the Issues, and Run Simulations.......... 123

38.   Copy-Paste... 154

39.   SQRA Report 167

    39.1   SQRA Report Format 167

    39.2   Front – Cover Page................................168

    39.3   Slide 1 – Purpose 169

    39.4   Slide 2 – Key Milestones 169

    39.5   Slide 3 – Primary Data..........................171

    39.6   Slide 4 – Schedule Quality Check......................172

    39.7   Slide 5 – Activities Selection Criteria.................173

    39.8   Slide 6 – Precaution on Report Distribution...175

    39.9   Slide 7 – Input Template.......................175

    39.10   Slide 8 – Participants 178

    39.11   Slide 9 – Static Critical Path 180

39.12   Slide 10 – Previous Sensitivity Analysis 182

39.13   Slide 11 – Top 10 Schedule Drivers 183

39.14   Slide 12 – Schedule Risk Analysis Summary ... 184

39.15   Slide 13 – Key Milestones/Activities 186

39.16   Slide 14 – Schedule Quality Assessment 187

39.17   Slide 15 – Schedule Check 190

39.18   Slide 16 – Disclaimer 192

39.19   Slide 17 – Errors and Warnings 193

39.20   Slides 18-19 – Probability Distribution 197

39.21   Slide 20 – Tornado Charts 201

39.22   Slide 20.1 Duration Sensitivity 202

39.23   Slide 20.2 Criticality Index 204

39.24   Slide 20.3 Cruciality 206

39.25   Slide 20.4 Schedule Sensitivity Index (SSI) 208

39.26   Slide 21 – Criticality Distribution Profile 210

39.27   Slide 22 – Criticality Path Report 212

39.28   Slide 22 – Distribution Analyzer 214

39.29   Slides 23-24 – Progress Curve & Histogram ... 216

39.30   Slides 25-26 – Labor Density and Complexity 218

39.31   Recommendation 223

40.   What You Have Learned 229

About the Author xxiii

Book Announcement! xxvii

List of Figures

Figure 1 - Components of a three-point estimate............................ 9
Figure 2 - Gantt dynamics of the 3-point estimate 10
Figure 3 – Probability (Air travel)... 11
Figure 4 – Collapsed bridge after a strong typhoon 13
Figure 5 - Rebels burned down company busses.......................... 16
Figure 6 - Flooding in Asia.. 18
Figure 7 – MC versus LH iteration 21
Figure 8 – Schedule contingency... 30
Figure 9 - Management of schedule quality 41
Figure 10 – Effects of changing calendars.................................. 47
Figure 11 – Time period calculation 49
Figure 12 - Fit for Purpose Approach 64
Figure 13 – Political Dates 84
Figure 14 - P10, P50, & P70 Probability Distribution................. 90
Figure 15 - Interview Sheet.. 97
Figure 16 – Three-point Range 113
Figure 17 - Project A Activity View 126
Figure 18 –P6 Activity View showing Ranges 127
Figure 19 – OPRA Import Settings Window............................. 128
Figure 20 – OPRA Import Log Dialogue Box.......................... 128
Figure 21 –Import Warning Log (Notepad text) 129
Figure 22 – Result of Import Check 130
Figure 23 –Translated Min, ML & Max Duration 131
Figure 24 –Translated Min, ML, & Max Duration.................. 133
Figure 25 –Import Setting\General... 134
Figure 26 – OPRA Import Setting\Tasks Tab 135
Figure 27 – OPRA Import Warning Report Log 136
Figure 28 – Check/Correct date setting.................................... 137
Figure 29 –Import Check 139
Figure 30 – Risk Analysis Dialogue Box.................................. 140
Figure 31 –Risk Analysis Options\Risk Data 141
Figure 32 –Risk Options\Analysis.. 141
Figure 33 – Risk Analysis Options\Warning............................ 142
Figure 34 – Risk Errors and Warning 1 143
Figure 35 –Risk Errors and Warning 2 143
Figure 36 –Risk Errors and Warning 3 144
Figure 37 – Calculation Status Box... 144

Figure 38 – Review OPRA Ranges if correct................................145
Figure 39 – Planning Unit...146
Figure 40 – Distribution Chart 1 147
Figure 41 –Distribution Chart 2 148
Figure 42 – Distribution Chart 3..149
Figure 43 – Distribution Analyzer 150
Figure 44 – Plan Options\Tim..151
Figure 45 – Schedule Options\Scheduling (OPRA)..................153
Figure 46 – Schedule Option\General (P6) 153
Figure 47 – Filter P6 Activities with duration range..................155
Figure 48 – Group and Sort 155
Figure 49 – Filtered and sorted activities.................................156
Figure 50 – Select ALL Activities 157
Figure 51 – COPY ALL Activities..158
Figure 52 – PASTE ALL Activities to Excel............................159
Figure 53 – Open the Schedule in OPRA 160
Figure 54 – Same Group & Sort Setting in OPRA 161
Figure 55 – Select and Copy the ranges from Excel.................162
Figure 56 – Select the first field and paste 163
Figure 57 – Pasted Duration Ranges on OPRA.........................164
Figure 58 – Triangle changed to Trigen 165
Figure 59 – Copy-Fill Trigen Distribution 166
Figure 60 – Cover Page 168
Figure 61 – Slide 1 Purpose Page 169
Figure 62 – Slide 2 Key Performance Milestones 170
Figure 63 – Slide 3 Primary Data...171
Figure 64 – Slide 4 Schedule Quality Check 172
Figure 65 – Slide 5 Filtering Criteria 174
Figure 66 – Slide 6 Filtering Criteria 175
Figure 67 – Input Worksheet 177
Figure 68 – Slide 8 Participants...180
Figure 69 – Slide 9 Static Critical Path...................................181
Figure 70 – Slide 10 Past Sensitivity Analysis 182
Figure 71 – Slide 11 Schedule Drivers....................................184
Figure 72 – Slide 12 SQRA Summary 186
Figure 73 – Slide 13 Key Milestones/Activities...........................187
Figure 74 – Slide 14 Quality Assessment Summary 189
Figure 75 – Slide 15 Schedule Check by OPRA........................191
Figure 76 – Slide 16 Analyst Disclaimer 192
Figure 77 – Slide 17 Errors and Warnings................................194
Figure 78 – Slide 18 Probability Distribution...............................198

Figure 79 – Slide 19 KMS 1130 (Close-up)......................................199
Figure 80 – Slide 19 KMS 1130 First Oil...200
Figure 81 – Slide 20 Tornado Chart 201
Figure 82 – Slide 20.1 Duration Sensitivity 203
Figure 83 – Slide 20.2 Criticality Index...205
Figure 84 – Slide 20.3 Cruciality (Full Chart) 207
Figure 85 – Slide 20.4 Schedule Sensitivity Index 209
Figure 86 – Slide 21 Criticality Distribution Profile.....................211
Figure 87 – Slide 22 Criticality Path Report..................................213
Figure 88 – Slide 22 Distribution Analyzer....................................215
Figure 89 – Slide 23 Construction Progress Chart 216
Figure 90 – Slide 24 Loading not aligned to Estimate...............217
Figure 91 – Slide 25 Work Area Plot Plan......................................220
Figure 92 – Slide 26 Labor Density and Complexity..................221

Preface

Schedule quantitative risk analysis (SQRA) is a process of calculating the overall probability or chance of completing a project on time and on budget. Quantification uses various approaches and methods. Duration ranging is the most popular and often referred to as the "traditional method" of schedule risk analysis.

It is simple, easy to understand, and it works.

New and upcoming project managers, leaders, planners and schedulers would love to wrap their heads around this special risk-based knowledge area. If you're one of them, you will enjoy reading this book.

The skills needed to perform SQRA has eluded many even as they try to learn how to effectively utilize the tool.

Relying on bits and pieces of information without understanding the quantitative process is a major sticking point. It is my intention to address them, giving you, the readers, full understanding of the subject. Isn't that what you want? Of course it is!

All must be reminded that management tools only facilitate the route and provide the quick indicators. The analysis resides mainly under the responsibility of a qualified risk-based project management practitioner like yourself.

There's no claim whatsoever that the tool will do or can do everything upon command. Knowledge of the process and understanding of the reference benchmarks employed and how they were formulated are very important in addition to being tool-savvy.

The tool is a vehicle to get you where you need to be, quicker and more accurate. One must use the tool to the "tool's right" for the project to succeed, to set it up properly for speedy and correct turnarounds less the common manual errors.

It was observed that some will pretend to know the quantitative tool and the processes involved, to the detriment of the company they worked in. There were some who slice and dice things that they really have no clear idea about.

It's time for all practitioners to sharpen the saw, to know exactly what needs to be done, why they are doing what they are doing, and finally for the more qualified persons to perform what's rightfully their area, the expertise that of schedule quantitative risk assessment.

Intellectual deceit and incompetence are not good. They are also bad combination. Ignorance is inexcusable and has to be treated with dedicated learning.

As such, I promised myself about three years ago that I would write a book on traditional SQRA. I have done it the shortest and simplest way so everyone can understand. Through this book, you can learn at your own pace.

Each Lesson uncovers certain aspect of risk analysis. It discusses fundamental knowledge in the Oracle Primavera Risk Analysis (OPRA) tool and related risk-based processes.

I want you, the readers, to confidently embark on schedule quantitative risk analysis without apprehension, doubt or anxiety by knowing you can do it right!

Traditional method of quantification is also called the three-point estimating method by many risk management practitioners. It looks at risk events and estimate uncertainties using three values of a given quantity such as duration, quantity, and cost.

To express uncertainty, the duration of each selected or risked activities is expressed as three-point range of values. During simulation, each duration becomes a variable, creating unique what-if schedule scenario for every iteration.

If one does a thousand iterations, it means that he did a thousand what-if project schedule scenarios. He has generated a thousand ways to look at the same schedule.

A thousand "what-ifs" can be more than enough to come up with a reliable forecast on probabilities and consequence concerning a specific deliverable. Three thousand to five thousand iterations improve preciseness of the result. Some can opt to choose a higher number.

Traditional method is applicable to cost risk analysis. It is excellent in capturing time-bound cost elements.

For example, equipment rental cost.

As the rental duration increases, the higher the total rental cost. We will require a cost-loaded schedule for us to come up with a generated probabilistic cost.

The three-point range of Duration and Cost represents the minimum, most likely, and maximum values. It means that each Duration or Cost of a risked activity is not a single point estimate.

The value can be anything from the estimated minimum,

crossing the most likely, and up to the estimated maximum.

The cost-loaded schedule model is not part of our in-depth discussion but will be mentioned where relevant and to some extent provide some clarity, but without going into too much details.

Rufran C. Frago

P. Eng., PMP®, CCP, PMI-RMP®, Author

Calgary, Alberta, Canada

Icons in this Book

TIP: This icon underlines some helpful information.

REMINDER: This icon reminds readers of key points to remember.

CAUTION: This icon alerts reader to consider negative consequence.

Acknowledgments

I trust and acknowledge the Lord with all my heart, remembering always not to put my confidence solely in my own understanding. He will direct my path (Proverbs 3:5-6). With Him, good things are possible. Thank you for giving me the power to complete this book. I pray that this humble contribution becomes useful to many through your help.

Thanks to my colleagues and peers across industries who spent valuable time performing cold-eyes reviews and professional edits of the manuscript. I have taken your inputs that made this book better serve the reader's needs.

My sincere appreciation to Armando Minia, Senior Technical Specialist @Bruce Power Nuclear Plant-Canada, Cecilio Besares, Professor @San Pablo College-Philippines, Menesse Richie M. Macababat, Senior Planning Engineer @Alcon (Nigeria) Limited-Nigeria, Noel Sanchez, Estimating Consultant @Sanchez Consulting-Canada, Perfecto Catelo- Sr. Technical Engineer, Plant Engineering Rapid Response Team @ Bruce Power Nuclear Plant-Canada, Stephen Odusanya, Mechanical Construction Engineer @Exxon-Mobil-Nigeria, Virgilio Monton, Senior Consultant @Turner and Townsend-Canada, and to Rachel Berry, Administrative Assistant/Free Lance Editor @Modus Strategic Solutions-Canada.

Rufran C. Frago P. Eng., PMP®, CCP, PMI-RMP®

Calgary, Alberta, Canada

1. Introduction

The primary objective in writing a separate and more detailed account of the traditional method of schedule quantitative risk analysis is to get more risk-based project/business management professionals, including planning, scheduling, estimating, and cost management practitioners to effectively run and operate the quantitative tool correctly, effectively, and with confidence in the shortest possible time, sans the struggle!

Risk-based processes accompany the instructional use of the tool to good effect. In that way, an integrated and holistic understanding of this simple analytical exercise is given more meaning. Tip, Reminder, and Warning icons will call reader's attention to essential information and heuristic intended to accelerate learning.

Some elements in this book were derived from the foundational principles discussed in my first book *Risk-based Management in the World of Threats and Opportunities: A Project Controls Perspective.* Relevant tips on risk-based planning and scheduling were added where they will give values. Essential excerpts were taken from my other two books where applicable and relevant: i.e. *How to Create a Good Quality P50 Risk-based Baseline Schedule,* and Plan *to Schedule, Schedule to Plan.*

The risk-based tools we'll be using throughout our lessons are the following:

- *Oracle Primavera Risk analysis V8, V8.7(OPRA)*
- *Primavera Project Management Professional (Primavera*

6.1 SP1, 6.2, 6.7 SP1, 6.7 SP2, SP4, & SP5 and higher version) V16/V17

OPRA is ancient compared to the new and upcoming risk analysis tool in the market today but it is quite powerful and simple to use. It has all what projects need to conduct a full-blown quantitative risk assessment.

It has the capability to do an integrated cost and schedule risk analysis, limited only by the knowledge and skill of its operator. Many risk management practitioners use OPRA. It is an essential tool in good and effective decision-making.

This book was structured in such a way that new OPRA Users with no experience can grab the control and operate the tool. The risk-based management processes are discussed simultaneously and in parallel with tool instructions. The combination will super-enhance the learning process, for one to become a successful schedule risk-analyst in the future.

If you have previous experience, it will come to you like a flood gate being opened, an "aha" moment will be found in every page. Not that it surprises you but because now you understood more, grasping risk-based management processes and terminology with ease and seeming familiarity.

At the end of your journey, you can import schedules to OPRA, successfully translate three-point duration ranges, perform schedule alignment checks, configure OPRA settings, adjust plan options, set task percentiles, change distribution function and run schedule risk analysis.

You will also become familiar with how to generate

probability distribution histograms, criticality distribution report, probability distribution analyzer, and tornadoes. To cap your new experience or review, I will slowly walk you through interpreting the results with you enjoying every moment.

Staying focused on the basics of traditional SQRA, we will not muddy the water with other approaches and methodologies that might bring confusion to new and upcoming practitioners.

I have excluded topics on the use of the risk register's qualitative/quantitative tables, risk scoring, risk breakdown structure (RBS), pre-mitigation, post mitigation, risk factors, and correlation. A project risk register is a tracking tabulation of identified risks for each project reflecting impact, probability, severity, action plan, and contingency.

Removing them from your immediate concerns for now will enable you to see the learning path clearly. The topics will be pursued soon but as part of a separate publication.

Do you know that schedule risk analysis calculates the overall probability of project completion? It looks at the overall uncertainty affecting the entire schedule, not just the effect on an activity or number of activities but overall.

It helps the project manager assess schedule achievability. It provides good perspectives, enabling him to choose the right schedule baseline.

Knowledge of the tool and the management processes involved lends to using resources more effectively.

Realistic budget and achievable schedule is no longer just a wish. It is a possibility and a reality.

2. Definitions

The term **User** in this book is the person using the Primavera or OPRA tool. He can be the risk analyst, planner, the scheduler, the Project Manager, or anyone.

The typical pre-requisites are project experience, knowledge of planning/scheduling processes, tool operating skills, and the capability to continuously learn. Without them, the person is not qualified to run the application. By the time you reach the last lesson, I want you to be a USER!

OPRA is an acronym for Oracle Primavera Risk Analysis tool. It was previously called PertMaster.

SQRA is the acronym for Schedule Quantitative Risk Analysis. It refers to the same process called SRA or Schedule Risk Analysis. The word quantification was added as a precise modifier that separates the analysis from the purely qualitative.

UDF is an acronym for Users Defined Field. It is a global code that can be created by any Primavera User given the proper security access. The schedule can be grouped and sorted using UDF and behave just like Global Activity Codes.

P6 is the Primavera Project Management scheduling tool.

An **Estimate** is a projected value of a certain quantities like labor workhours, various measurements, length of pipes, number of elbows, fittings, nuts and bolts using available scientific methods.

Deterministic Schedule is a schedule that represents a single point time estimate. Each of the task carries a single duration. Original project schedule is a deterministic schedule. The schedule imported or translated to OPRA for risk simulation is deterministic. This schedule has fixed duration and can only give the following information.

- Predicts a single completion date and/or cost
  Examples:

    o Company A will spend USD$5M this year.

    o This project will take 13 months to complete.

- Uses single value for activity duration and/or cost
  Examples:

    o Our piling activity will take 20 days and cost us USD$100,000.

    o "Five days to mobilize our contractors," said the Field Engineer.

- Do not take uncertainty and risk into account, assuming 100 % probability
  Examples:

    o Declaring "Company A will spend USD$5M this year is a statement of absolute certainty" compared to "Company A might spend USD3M to USD$7M this year. Most likely, it will be USD$5M."

3. SQRA

Several scheduling software, programs, and applications in the market have limited capabilities catering to schedule risk analysis.

Primavera Project Management (P6) stand-alone application is one of the few that has a built-in risk analysis tool called OPRA.

This risk analysis tool can also be a separate installation, accessed through a separate and distinct icon.

This is the reason why several other upcoming applications has started to offer specialized risk analysis module in their existing platform. Deltek Acumen Risk is one of them, User friendly, high resolution graphics, attractive colors, with plenty of bells and whistles.

Schedule quantitative risk analysis calculates the overall probability or chance of completing a project on time and on budget. Quantification process uses various distribution profiles but the most popular is Triangular and Trigen. We will deal only with these two profiles going forward.

Duration and costs three-point range represent the minimum, most likely, and maximum values. Contemplating duration, it means that each duration of risked activity is being evaluated no longer as a single point estimate but a three-point.

To express uncertainty, each duration is expressed as a range. During simulation, each duration becomes a variable, creating a unique what-if schedule scenario for every iteration. It is applicable to the cost element as well if the schedule is cost-loaded.

A cost-loaded risk-model will not be a part of the subsequent discussion but will be mentioned in some ways relevant without going into details.

The three points estimate method is what many call the *traditional method* of quantification. It can look solely on risk events or purely estimating uncertainties where relevant. The complete approach is to consider the combination of the two elements (Figure 1 and Figure 2).

Imagine cable pulling work during the winter months of December to February.

One can quickly conclude that since the work will occur in winter months, the job might take longer than if the activity occurs during the summer months of June to August. The activity might require hoarding, heating, new storage arrangement, special equipment, additional resources, and expertise.

A good project risk analyst sees the cascade of work, the forecasted dates, the timeline on which it sits, and discerns the degree of uncertainty affecting each of the work package by analyzing the project schedule.

Accurate modeling is required. It is only possible if the project uses a good quality schedule as specimen of quantification.

This important caveat is needed to satisfy the expectation of a useful result.

It is good practice to consider positive and negative risks

as equally important. Uncertainties are captured using risk factors and their accompanying ranges. Risk events come from the risk register and issue log.

Always consider at least two types of risks. One is the inherent risks, often referred to as systemic risks. The second one is project-specific risks.

Don't put the book down now. Just continue reading a bit more and I will lead you by the hand to revisit the fundamentals of risk, probability, and impact.

There are enough materials for you to truly appreciate qualitative and quantitative risk analysis.

Check out the collated preview on schedule analytics and generated reports.

An explanation of the key benefits associated with the proper management of risks highlights the practical application of risk-based management using schedule quantification as a window of opportunity.

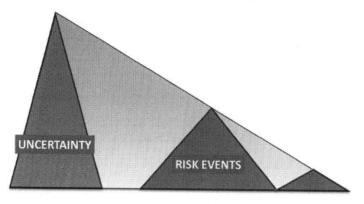

Figure 1 - Components of a three-point estimate

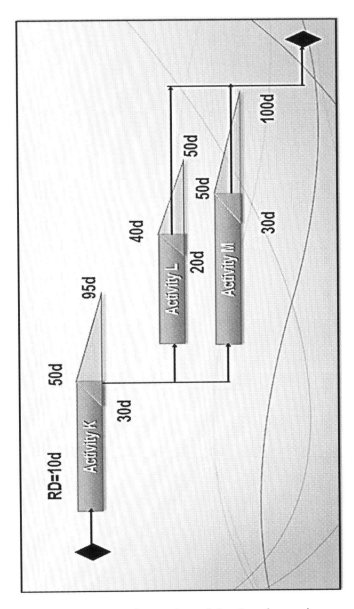

Figure 2 - Gantt dynamics of the 3-point estimate

4. Visualizing Risk

Mark is boarding a plane and heard one passenger in front of him remarks jokingly that the chance of the plane reaching its destination is 50% (Figure 3).

It is just a joke to him because he is a risk practitioner. The statement demonstrates the probability component of risk.

Figure 3 – Probability (Air travel)

Probability is the certainty or uncertainty of something happening.

Since risk is widely known to be the effect of uncertainty on objective, the objective of reaching the destination is only 50% certain. Another way of looking at it is by saying it is 50% uncertain.

What can be some of the possible consequences a passenger might be thinking? A new passenger might be anxious and entertain the thought of the plane crashing.

A less experienced passenger might entertain the thought that plane might be diverted to another place due to some emergency or threat.

A more experienced passenger might say that no real risk is present and that the plane will reach the destination on time.

The perspective of an observer depends largely on the specific risk identified, plus his knowledge and experience on the subject.

5. Visualizing Impact

Impact points to the possible consequence if the identified risk happens. It is the occurrence of an event resulting from the risk being realized. Figure 4 shows a collapsed bridge (Photo by Bullit Marquez, 2014), the consequence of flood water surge brought about by a strong typhoon and heavy rains that went on for days.

Figure 4 – Collapsed bridge after a strong typhoon

When the risk materialized, technically, it is no longer a risk but a problem. If not solved within some reasonable time frame, the problem will persist. By that time, it would be an issue.

Projects must manage risks in order to avoid, prevent, and mitigate possible problems and issues that can result if they occur. A "realized-risk" cost money, can damage reputation, might incur loss of human lives, of resources, and in numerous instances, business closures.

Let us say the risk of the bridge collapsing was identified a year before. This present-day problem was but a risk in the past and now, it is not. It became real!

If we go back into the past a bit more, you will discover that the risk was the result of another risk. The risk identified today was the result of the risk you were not able to avoid or mitigate in the past.

The risk of flood water surge cannot be avoided but installing surge breakers would have mitigated its impact, saving the bridge.

Another example was a key issue discovered a few years before the time. There was indication of soil erosion around the bridge foundation. The continuous yearly exposure of the bridge foundation from previous storms and floods has taken its toll. Some people complained that the local government in-charge has not done enough to mitigate the risk.

The bridge finally went down during the last storm. The consequence of the bridge finally failing brought other major consequence such as death, property damage, disruption to commerce and education, transport issues, health problems, and many others.

It brought adverse safety, health, social, and economic impact to everyone in the area and nearby places. Definitely, this was a major setback to the flow of commerce that comes in and out of that province.

The situation could have been avoided if the government had reviewed the risk register and promptly addressed the reported risk.

The charred remains of the busses shown in Figure 5 are the consequence of an insurgent's attack against a company operating in one of the developing country in Asia. It is a coercive tactic of collecting tax from businesses.

Management stopped the morning run of the bus carrying employees to work. The group forced everyone to disembark and later doused the busses with gasoline. They then ignited the vehicle using rocket propelled grenades (RPGs).

The plant safety officer was aware of the threat but dismissed the probability of the event occurring.

Fortunately, there was no casualty.

The key risk indicator (KRI) is the fact that there were numerous sightings of the group within a ten kilometers radius of the plant six to nine months before the burning incident happened.

The burning incident disrupted bus service to and from work. It incurred additional cost, forcing plant management to add better surveillance infrastructure, to hire additional security guards, and to deploy several military escorts. Some employees resigned for fear of their life.

Rumors also circulated that the company had succumbed to the demands of the group's progressive taxation to prevent further losses. Management provided additional pay as incentives to employees, hoping to relieve them some of their fears. Still the remaining employees productivity decreased due to uncertainty concerning personal safety.

This type of risk is quite common in many countries of the world and companies learn to manage their way through, one way or another.

Figure 5 - Rebels burned down company busses

6. Visualizing Probability

Probability is a measure of uncertainty of the consequence. If the consequence is zero, then the logical risk consideration is gone. There is no risk because the consequence will not happen. If the possibility is greater than zero, then the consequence might happen. The greater the probability, the greater the chance of the subject consequence happening.

One way to visualize risks is to look at the picture of a situation or the situation itself. Hold it in front of you and imagine that you are there. If you are in there, ask yourself why? What is your purpose of being there? Are you there in behalf of an enterprise? Are you there to help or to document what is happening?

What are the boundaries dictating your actions? What can you give? Are you a neutral observer whose interest is for the general good? Figure 6 shows portions of a flooded metropolitan. What do you see? What is it to you?

If you are on a sturdy boat taking this picture, the possibility is small that you will consequently end up in the water. In any case, that is still a risk you might want to consider. The fact that some people are in dirty floodwater, conjure up the risks of diseases eventually contracted by them. You can calculate that such a probability is high.

Thinking about risk in terms of probability should be easy enough if you think about the consequence within the framework of your objectives or the objectives of the entity you represent.

Figure 6 - Flooding in Asia

7. Risk Simulation

Monte Carlo (MC) simulation is the name given to a method of analysis that runs iterations to produce a statistical result.

This is opposed to deriving a function that would give the required result (often an almost impossible task in anything but the simplest of plans).

Latin Hypercube (LH) simulation is a stratified method of sampling a distribution that gives outcomes nearer the theoretical values of the input distribution with less iteration.

The two are both simulations but they do it in different way. New risk analyst mistakenly calls all simulation as Monte Carlo.

It is not a big deal to those who are not deeply intertwined with the risk analysis process. Some risk professionals will call your attention and make the correction if you use Latin Hypercube in simulation but keeps calling it Monte Carlo.

It will not drastically change the result, yet I am mentioning it here, so you know. I do not want you to go become a manager calling one process another.

It is not a big deal to those who are not deeply intertwined with the risk analysis process. Some risk professionals will call your attention and make the correction if you use Latin Hypercube in simulation and keep calling it Monte Carlo. It would not drastically change the result. However, a manager should be precise with terminology of process.

The efficacy of Monte Carlo (MC) or Latin Hypercube (LH) has nothing to do with the type of model, (e.g. cost estimate or schedule).

It is practically just a question of how much time it takes to reach stability and coming up with the results.

Generally, LH stabilizes results quicker than MC. However, a Monte Carlo simulation of a schedule with few activities could stabilize quicker than a Latin Hypercube simulation of a cost estimate or schedule having many input ranges.

Monte Carlo takes the three points estimate representation of each activity (represented by the triangle) and divides it into equal segments.

The tool samples a random segment in each iteration. Randomness makes it less likely but possible that the same sample segment is selected more than once.

Each iteration is a "what-if" scenario of the project. One thousand iterations are like looking at 1000 project scenarios.

This means that a thousand iterations are like looking at the same project one thousand times, with a different situation each time.

Five thousand iterations are like looking at the same project using five thousand times what-ifs. The value of each three points range contributes to the overall probability distribution.

Latin Hypercube does the same, but without repeating previously sampled values. Each sample is unique. To conclude, the black box sampling method provides a better representation of the risk model. It is also relatively faster even though we are really talking only time units in seconds.

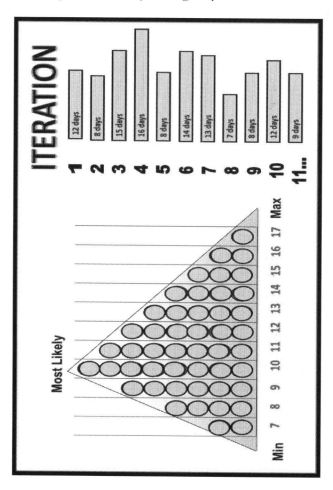

Figure 7 – MC versus LH iteration

8. Tools and Techniques

The PMBOK Guide briefly explains the tools that can be used for qualitative risk assessment.

An aspiring risk manager can use risk probability and impact assessment, probability and impact matrices, risk data quality assessment, risk categorization, risk urgency assessment, and expert judgment (PMI, 2013).

The result of quantitative risk analysis depends largely on the process of data gathering and representation techniques. The way a risk analyst gathers, groups, and interprets his data ultimately affects the quality of the inputs and the results.

Did he gather his inputs using Delphi technique or facilitated meeting? Did the inputs come from frontline disciplines or their managers? Maybe, their manager's manager? Perhaps, an outsider?

Were the inputs given freely and honestly without bias? Did he involve a full complement of knowledgeable resources? Was there any important stakeholder who did not participate? Did the individual resource get enough time to review the schedule? Were they familiar with the risk involved and the scope?

From experience, some members of the team are more vocal than others. Sometimes, a senior manager may influence the cost and/or schedule input one way or another without any question from other passive participants, resulting in a largely biased and erroneous risk output.

There are so many questions to consider that can gauge how well data gathering went and that is just one segment of the whole story.

Next step is how to represent data in the model. This will not be overly complicated as we will be discussing only the traditional method of risk analysis.

It is expected that everyone who provided the duration ranges understood the proper way of framing their input values.

By doing so, there will be no unnecessary skewness brought about by a wrong premise. If all participating members understand what the organization's risk appetite is, the risk analysis process becomes less subjective.

Knowing the degree of uncertainty, the organization can better decide the risks it is willing to take in anticipation of the rewards (PMI, 2013). This information gives the participating disciplines the confidence to call out the more realistic three-point estimate because ranges are viewed in the right context.

The risk workshop facilitator must see to it that all resource persons stand on the same footing, seeing the same perspective of the schedule risk landscape.

If the schedule risk appetite of the company is represented by P50, then everyone must understand its relevance.

They must know that the result of the SQRA will use this P50 criteria to calculate schedule contingency. The risk analyst evaluates schedule risks against such criteria to determine appropriate risk treatment.

Quantitative risk analysis and modelling techniques can use any tool specially designed for the purpose.

Project management professionals in any industry, be it in construction and engineering, have probably heard or use the tools such as OPRA (previously Pertmaster), Crystal Ball, @Risk, the Decision Tools, Neural Tools, Deltek Acumen Risk, and similar others.

9. SQRA Benefits

Since schedule quantitative risk analysis (SQRA) was designed to uphold baseline cost and schedule, it will also support the project to successfully deliver high quality result in safety. The risk analysis tool can be utilized to accelerate or decelerate the control schedule, perhaps to reduce costs on both counts and still achieve main objectives.

By identifying the top schedule drivers, project managers have a better chance of successfully managing the projects through hoops and loops of execution. Each important milestone becomes available for inspection and assessment in terms of probability. The project will increase the likelihood of achieving objectives. Identifying the principal risks also reveals hidden critical paths to work on.

Given this, the project can work on a formula geared to reducing risk exposures. Scope and contract management becomes more effective and less subjective. It can give the project team a better appreciation of schedule achievability.

Assuming valve delivery is one of the long lead item included in the critical path to complete the piping installation and the cost of expediting delivery, air freight may be considered.

If the delivery of the valves would result in significant cost or schedule delay to the project, the Project Team should include to the estimate the cost to mitigate the delivery of the valve on time. Some example: paying premium or selecting the vendor with the shortest delivery time, Air freight, or overtime premium to expedite the delivery, assigning a dedicated expeditor to the project, etc.

Projects can put available resources together and increase confidence by creating a more realistic budget and schedule, using the quantitative results as reckoning points. Using SQRA, you can help the project be proactive, improving its capability to identify schedule threats and opportunities.

Criticality becomes dynamic and more valuable source of information. Schedule risk drivers become realistic, more pronounced and easily identifiable.

It is also easy to validate driving activities, opening the best opportunities to effectively address them.

Having a handle on the project's most important deliverables improves controls. A good and steady grasp on the steering wheel improves stakeholder's trust and confidence.

Who knows? You might even be successful increasing your company stock price whenever you want to!

10. Contingency

Quantitative risk analysis generates distribution charts. Visual illustration of schedule contingency using **Figure 8** information and chart will give a better appreciation of the concept.

Schedule data date   = 14-Aug-2017

P50 Date   = 05-Aug-2018

P70 Date   = 08-Aug-2018

Deterministic Date   = 25-Jul-2018 @ <P1

Project risk standard   = P50

We measure risk dates differences from the deterministic end date. The difference between XYZ Upgrader Project Risk Standard P50 and the deterministic date is termed schedule contingency (Frago, July 2010).

Looking at the distribution chart, there are thirteen days, or ~1.5 weeks schedule contingency between the deterministic date of July 25, 2018 and the August 5, 2018 P50 date.

Determining the value to add or subtract from the base schedule (or cost) to achieve the desired probability of under run is straightforward.

The amount of time (or money) added or subtracted from the base schedule is termed as schedule (or cost) contingency (Wendling, 1999).

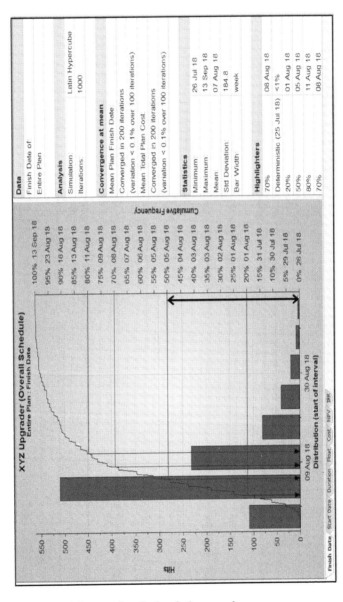

Figure 8 – Schedule contingency

30

11. Duration Range

Everyone in the risk management community knows what schedule quantitative risk analysis is. It is what most of us in project management call the traditional method of quantification. One day, I decided to ask a group of subject matter experts this.

"What do you think is the best approach to duration ranging?"

I have done and facilitated so many three-point activity duration estimating sessions that I have already lost count. Regardless of how many, though, I still ask myself, "Am I doing the three-point estimate correctly?"

There is a growing opinion from some risk management professionals that the "duration range" should only consider estimation of uncertainties, not risk events. Let us take the activity called "piling installation". It is an activity with 20 days duration. Most probably, it will take 20 days, but it can be 25 days at maximum and 18 days at minimum.

This three-point spread is solely because of estimating uncertainty.

This means that the activity should not be tied to a risk event (or events) taking place. According to them, risk events should be considered separately using the risk register (risk scoring).

Duration ranging should stick within the range and averages of the work itself based on normal conditions and not on assumptions of abnormal conditions taking place.

Relative Values between Three Points

How about duration ranging? How should we monitor the validity of the three-point estimate? Should the risk analyst allow the following flawed values?

- Most likely duration equals minimum duration; i.e. ML =MIN
- Most likely duration equals maximum duration; i.e. ML=MAX
- Most Likely Duration is less than Minimum Duration; i.e. ML < MIN
- Most Likely is greater than Maximum Duration; i.e. ML > MAX
- Most Likely is equal to Minimum and Maximum Duration; i.e. ML=MIN=MAX
- Most Likely is different from the Remaining Duration; i.e. ML NE RD

These relative values are quite common when facilitating a risk session or running the risk analysis itself. Default Most Likely (ML) value of each activity considered is equal to the activity's remaining duration.

The default was borne out of the basic principle of schedule development that calls for the schedule to represent the "most likely."

In many cases, projects end up giving any of the numerous flawed inputs stated above. When this happens, the activity on focus is not a P50, or the Most Likely.

When ML is not equal to RD, depending on the differential value, and the frequency, the schedule is saying whether it is aggressive or lax.

Once all the values are in, the risk analysis tool runs the simulation. It will calculate the inputs versus the network backdrop, providing the result or generate either a warning, or an error.

The errors and/or warnings usually boil down to preceding items 1 to 6.

A subject matter resource who inputs a value that has ML=MIN is trying to say that the remaining duration is flawed and does not represent the expected value of P50.

When he brings the minimum value to equal the most likely value, he is saying that finishing the activity on time using the remaining duration has less probability.

It will be a bigger challenge than when the ML stays as is, and the minimum value opens to the left of any specific duration range.

He thinks that the remaining duration of the activity is the earliest possible duration. As such, the remaining duration of the activity is nowhere near the most likely deterministic duration value.

Conversely, when ML=MAX, it means that there is no way the activity will complete later than what is shown in the remaining duration of the activity.

It can also be interpreted the Most Likely value as too pessimistic and needs to be recalibrated to a lesser value. The facilitator must clarify from the subject matter experts

(SME) the rationale and act accordingly.

By saying so, the project is assuring that the deterministic value is the same as maximum.

Does this make sense? Something is not quite right if one thinks about it for a moment.

If two of the three values were equal, would it still be a 3-point range?

What is a good perspective?

Are we going to allow this?

If yes, why should we allow this?

Many risk analysts still consider the right triangle distribution as a valid distribution. Fortunately, the SQRA tool can successfully do the calculation.

In other words, there is technically no problem. The facilitator should try to avoid such a distribution scenario because it is not a good reflection of the possible ranges and can be self-defeating. Such distribution is unrealistic and better deemed impossible.

Items 3 and 4 will come out as error. Calculation will stop. The Most Likely value lying outside the confines of minimum and maximum values is unacceptable. Calculation will not proceed unless the issue fixed.

Calculation stops because values relationships do not make sense.

Again, when the Most Likely duration equals the Minimum and Maximum or ML=MIN=MAX, the warning message comes up. This kind of entry is the same as no entry at all if Remaining Duration is equal to Most Likely or RD=ML. Now, I'm sure you won't forget this simple rule.

Since there is no duration range provided, it has practically no input to provide. You can ignore the warnings.

A popular distribution is called the TRIGEN (P10/P90). This is a distribution profile where the minimum represents, for example a P10 and your maximum a P90.

The calculation brings into consideration what risk practitioners call "outliers", values which describes the remaining 10% outside the P10/P90 points.

When a subject matter expert provides duration input ranges based on their experience, the assumption considered is that their minimum and maximum value inputs are not true reflections of the actual minimum and maximum. Rationale:

Even the experts have not experienced the real minimum and maximum values in their lifetime. To compensate for the blind spot, we opt for P10/P90 to consider outliers.

12. Three-Point Estimate

It will be beneficial for anyone performing a three-point estimate to review the information and data quality of the following documents:

- Basis of Estimate
- Detailed Estimate
- Estimate Summary

This provides a good understanding on how the duration of an activity or work package came about. It is mandatory that the facilitator is familiar with the estimate, because crosschecking the resource inputs is essential.

Removing the unfounded biases during duration ranging will address some of the dreaded systemic schedule risk.

Note the relevant project stage or phase and how they can help validate the duration estimate and the ranges. Be familiar with the estimate classes adopted for the stage.

Understand that knowledge of the estimate basis is a big plus; e.g. number of crew per day, number of hours per day, composition of mixed crews, work assumptions, work strategies, rules for fabrication and construction, and others.

Avoid Double Dipping

Double dipping is a common problem in three-point estimating involving risk event consideration.

The participating disciplines and stakeholders tend to come up with risk events already captured in the risk register. The risk analyst should be constantly aware of this. In addition to the documents listed in Section 12 is the latest and up to date project risk register.

The problem happens when risk events that were qualified and quantified using the risk register are now again part of the discussion in SQRA.

Only those risks not found in the risk register, or in the risk register but not yet evaluated, are best included in the schedule risk analysis.

Three common methods of quantifications:

- By identifying new and relevant risks and incorporating them into the approved risk matrix table of the risk analysis tool. Tying and correlating each risk to the impacted activities or work packages follows.

- Using traditional approach or commonly called three-point estimating. Review and simulation of specially selected activities according to agreed-to criteria using duration range as input.

- Record the risks considered in a common project register and do separate empirical calculations to come up with the dollar or duration value.

13. Data Quality

The correctness, accuracy, completeness, and usefulness of a Schedule Quantitative Risk Analysis (SQRA) shall depend heavily on the quality of planning data used for input or plainly, the quality of the project schedule.

As I have highlighted in the first part of this write-up, a good quality schedule is required to come up with good quantitative results. It is the root of it all. Good quality begets good management that begets good result.

I have written a guide called "How to Prepare for Schedule Quantitative Risk Analysis" which focuses particularly on the ready for SQRA criteria (Frago, 2013) where I discussed comprehensively the effects of schedule quality on the process of quantitative risk analysis.

The consequences of a poor-quality schedule are practically endless if one wants to be specific about it. If unaddressed, the schedule remains counter-intuitive, disconnected, and/or disjointed, resulting in poor project management and control.

Low quality produces a flawed schedule not fit for quantitative risk analysis, as it will produce incorrect probability calculations. It will also most likely generate the wrong critical path, influencing the project to focus on wrong activities.

Miscommunication and communication breakdown are two known consequences. A schedule with missing scope is inaccurate and will aggravate the problems caused by missing inputs, both to the plan and the schedule. The recycling of wrong and missing information is an issue that management can do without.

A poor schedule has a negative effect on work productivity. It goes against achievability.

Condoning a deficient schedule is definitely the wrong planning and scheduling strategy, producing unclear results and unfulfilled expectations because the project team loses the opportunity to manage the project better.

Other consequences:

- Increases the threat to project objectives

- Creates confusions

- Work strategy can become ineffective

- Flaws in resource distribution analysis

- Managing resources becomes more challenging

- Resource leveling will be in error

- Generates false risk and performance indicators

- Wrong progress report

- Unable to assess scope and achievability accurately

- Project misalignment

- Scope is less clear

- Missing scope, schedule is incomplete

It is a sad paradox to conclude that many ill-prepared

project schedules are victims of time constraints. A schedule is supposed to manage time effectively, yet, developing one to the right quality becomes impossible in favor of expediency.

"We have to submit the baseline tomorrow for our gate review. There's no time to address all the schedule's flaws and inherent risks. This will do," says the project control manager.

Consequently, a poor-quality schedule becomes the project's Achilles heel. Too bad! Avoid the mentality of "it's good enough!" One must strive for excellence whenever possible.

Figure 9 - Management of schedule quality

There are several semi-automatic quality assessment tools available in the industry today. They can help the project manager gain more insight into the very fiber of their schedule.

A product called Deltek-Acumen Fuse, for example, can provide a powerful dashboard style presentation of schedule quality based on any in-house or industry standard benchmark criteria (Frago, R., 2013. How to Understand Acumen Fuse Score. Slideshare).

Anyone can also assess schedule quality satisfactorily using P6 groups and filter functions. This will be briefly discussed in one of the sub-topics later.

14. Schedule Validation

Validating the project schedule is essential before anyone embarks into full-fledged SQRA. The schedule must be the right sample.

This touches on the significance of good schedule quality as a decent starting point towards schedule risk quantification.

Upon quality validation and subsequent SQRA, the project must approve a baseline for execution.

Ideally, all the stakeholders have to vet and sign the baseline schedule.

If this is not possible, then all the most influential and powerful schedule stakeholders must complete the sign-off.

The project stakeholder register will provide the information as to who should be involved.

Ideally, it should have the information as who among the stakeholders have more influence, the power to decide.

It will be very contentious if any schedule stakeholder argues that the analysis is unacceptable because the summarized project schedule does not reflect the detailed schedule.

15. Calendars

The calendar is a contentious element of a schedule. The challenge here is that we are often not talking about one or two calendars. The project, through the schedulers, has a nasty habit of creating numerous calendars.

I have reviewed one major project a few years back that had 11 calendars. The contractors prepared the sub-projects separately, thinking that each one will have a different calendar. The good thing is that, upon closer inspection, five of the eleven calendars were practically the same.

Upon conversion of the five to a singular calendar, I still must convince the project that the remaining seven calendars were just too much. Fortunately, the project finally decided to use just two calendars.

Too many calendars can complicate the schedule. The number of calendars must be just right. Streamlining them is the best way and it simplifies the risk analysis process greatly.

Many planners/schedulers do not take good care of their schedule calendars. They take on a new project schedule without inspecting the attributes of the assigned calendars. Planners and schedulers should check for completeness of the calendar attributes; e.g. holidays, non-work days, work days, and others. Sometimes, the calendar runs short, the attributes of which was not specified up to the duration of the project.

Error in calendar assignments makes progress and duration calculation erroneous. The wrong calendar affects all the activities that should have had a different calendar.

Look at the example in **Figure 10**. The top activity window shows 8h day/5d week assigned to engineering activities and 10h day/5d week assigned to construction activities. The lead planning person found out that both engineering and construction were each using the wrong calendar. When the right calendars were assigned to the activities, schedule dates and the durations changed accordingly.

Experience indicates that more often than not, the time period calculation was wrong, creating wrong dates and duration.

You have to be aware of this type of error most especially if you represent the client side.

Sad to say, some contractors intentionally use this simple configuration to go around sponsor company's best interest. Exercise due diligence. Check what is in the contract to make sure that the assigned activity calendars are right.

Assignment errors are easy to detect but time period configuration errors need closer inspection to notice. One must check calendar exceptions and unusual entry. An example of this was one calendar designating all Wednesdays to 9 hours instead of 10 hours per day. It was odd, so the risk analyst flagged the mistake. It was promptly corrected.

Exercise caution when importing contractor schedules into your company's scheduling database. You see, some of these external schedules will inherit global calendars from their source database that might be in violation of contract agreement. Time periods set values for weeks, months, and years need to be reviewed and validated. Make sure that calculation is correct. You must understand the intention of assigned calendars.

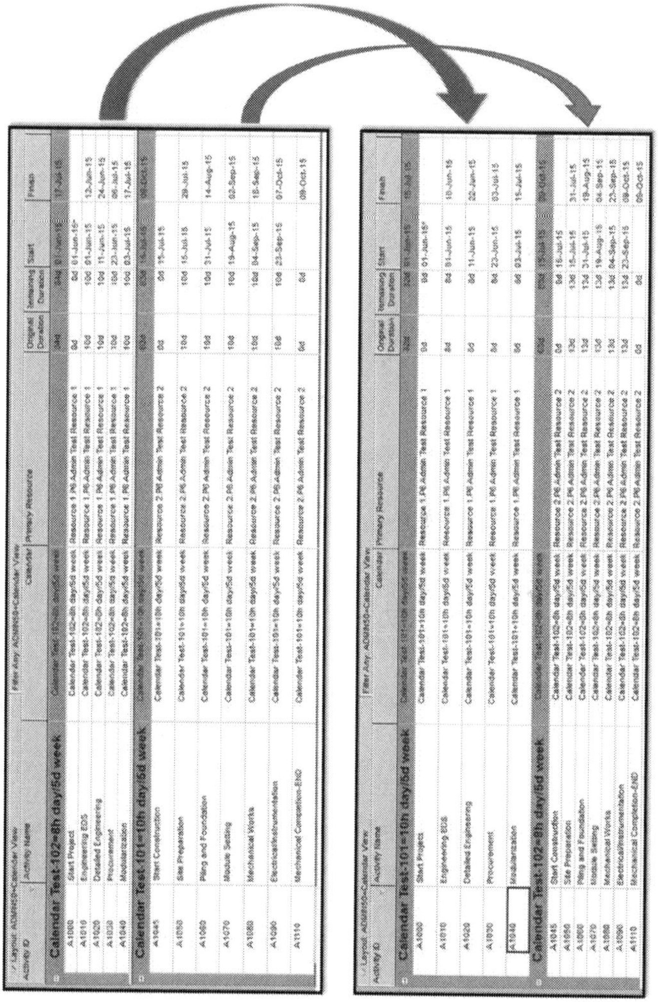

Figure 10 – Effects of changing calendars

Primavera calculates and stores time unit values in hourly increments. When you display or enter data in time unit fields in increments other than hours, the Project Management module converts the data based on the Hours per Time Period settings.

Conversely, if the User enters time units in increments other than hours, the Hours per Time Period settings are used to convert these input values to hours for the scheduling database calculation and storage.

To display time unit data accurately, the User should set the correct Hours per Time Period values in each of the calendar. This is of course, on top of the calendar being assigned to the right activity and resources.

The proposed time period configuration based on the type of calendar is shown in **Figure 11.** The project should have this table available to all planners/schedulers

Calendar	D/W	D/M	D/Y	Hours/Day	Hours/Week	Hours/Month	Hours/Year
4 Days Calendar	4.00	17.14	205.71	5.00	20.00	85.71	1,028.57
	4.00	17.14	205.71	11.00	44.00	188.57	2,262.86
5 Days Calendar	5.00	21.43	257.14	8.00	40.00	171.43	2,057.14
	5.00	21.43	257.14	9.00	45.00	192.86	2,314.29
	5.00	21.43	257.14	10.00	50.00	214.29	2,571.43
	5.00	21.43	257.14	12.00	60.00	257.14	3,085.71
6 Days Calendar	6.00	25.71	308.57	10.00	60.00	257.14	3,085.71
	6.00	25.71	308.57	12.00	72.00	308.57	3,702.86
7 Days Calendar	7.00	30.00	360.00	8.00	56.00	240.00	2,880.00
	7.00	30.00	360.00	10.00	70.00	300.00	3,600.00
	7.00	30.00	360.00	12.00	84.00	360.00	4,320.00
	7.00	30.00	360.00	10.50	73.50	315.00	3,780.00
	7.00	30.00	360.00	11.50	80.50	345.00	4,140.00
	7.00	30.00	360.00	20.00	140.00	600.00	7,200.00
	7.00	30.00	360.00	24.00	168.00	720.00	8,640.00

Calendar	~/W	~/M	~/Y	Hours/Day	Hours/Week	Hours/Month	Hours/Year
7 days Calendar	1.00	4.35	52.14	10.00	70.19	304.17	3,650.00
	1.00	4.35	52.14	11.50	80.72	349.79	4,197.50
10 x 4 Calendar	0.50	2.17	26.07	10.00	50.14	217.26	2,607.14
	0.50	2.17	26.07	24.00	120.33	521.43	6,257.14
9 x 5 Calendar	0.50	2.17	26.07	10.00	45.12	195.54	2,346.43
14 x 7 Calendar	0.33	1.45	17.38	10.00	46.79	202.78	2,433.33
	7.00	30.00	365.00	10.00	70.00	300.00	3,650.00

Figure 11 – Time period calculation

16. Baseline Schedule

 Baseline schedule should never be developed and built in isolation. It should have the inputs of all stakeholders and must represent the "most likely" schedule with no built-in risk. Doing this will limit vulnerability to double-dipping risk inputs.

One should remember that risk is something that might or might not happen in the future.

The project watches for triggers ushering the schedule risks. Triggers are symptoms that the risk is about to become a reality. It is very important because it lends the project some time to execute the response plan.

Do not consider risks in creating the baseline. The baseline shall reflect only what the project intends to happen. The schedule baseline is the true reflection of the plan.

Every risk has a trigger before it happens, and that is the only time the risk action owner should activate the corresponding response plan.

A decision has to be made whether to avoid, transfer, mitigate, share, or accept the risk if it's a threat or to exploit, share, enhance, or accept if the risk is an opportunity.

For additional clarity about these strategies, see PMBOK 6th Edition. Chapter 11, page 441 - 446, Section 11.5.2 Plan Risk Responses: Tools and Techniques (4th Edition, Chapter 11, page 303-305, Section 11.5.2 Plan Risk Responses: Tools and Techniques).

17. Schedule Filter

One of the more popular approaches used prior to embarking into duration ranging was to filter the schedule's critical and normal activities. Identifying about 300 to 500 activities in the process is common.

From these, the risk analyst filter out activities with relatively short duration such as those with RD<=3D.

To exclude less critical activities, the filter is changed, adjusted to define the schedule's degree of criticality.

The following can be set:

TF<10D, or perhaps TF<15D, whichever will give a count of about 150 to 300 activities, (or whatever acceptable representative statistical target number of activities suits the project).

All of these will depend largely on the level of schedule.

There is also a danger that some activities will not fall into the set criteria.

Review the results diligently as these activities might have high potential to change drastically because of risk factors and end up influencing the result.

18. Static Path

The issue I always have in the back of my mind using the filter approach of identifying critical paths is this:

 Critical paths are more dynamic in nature than static. Constantly changing with each schedule update even activities with high criticality can switch path. Some might even end up as non-critical.

What we can filter from our P6 schedule are static critical paths. They are practically just a snapshot of the path in time.

That snapshot is equivalent to a singular iteration run, using our risk analysis tool. Never rely on this indicator with blind confidence. Always crosscheck with periodic schedule risk analysis.

The overwhelming importance given by many project managers on static path is one of the reasons why they fail to have a good handle of their projects.

They fail to note down that just like the dates, the path is deterministic. It is good only during the moment of inspection and does not offer even a short standing influence on the overall deliverables.

If this path is never changing, then project managers can bet their career on it.

Since the path will change sometime along the way, one

can merely pick any 200 activities at random and say they can be critical the next time around.

What a downer!

It seems very ineffective and absurd to focus on the critical path produced by a singular run or a singular iteration.

Know that running the schedule risk analysis is the far better method of identifying schedule criticality.

SQRA simulates all scenarios. Since the number of iteration equals the number of what-ifs, a 5000-iteration equals 5000 what-ifs.

One iteration is equal to one scenario.

Five thousand (5,000) iterations is like looking at the same project but in various scenarios, 5,000 times.

19. Integrated Analysis

Integrated assessment is a must! Proper schedule risk quantification requires an integrated schedule that has all the needed elements under consideration. All activities have to be part of the same deterministic network during calculation with all essential and correct relationships preserved.

How can you tell that a schedule lacks integration?

One major indicator of a schedule that is not integrated is the presence of external links. If you find an external link, it signifies a separate schedule lying outside the realm of your schedule risk model. As much as possible all the interconnected schedules are present or represented in the integrated model.

Another indicator is the presence of open ends. Open ends such as missing predecessors and/or successors cause time and risk analysis calculations to be erroneous. The greater the number of open ends the more unreliable the result of quantification becomes. An open end is an indication of missing scope, incomplete or missing planning inputs. All open ends must be re-tied properly.

If it is impossible to bring all scopes under one schedule, the external link must be understood in such a way so that they are represented well in the model. Otherwise, the analyst must bring all the external schedules into the same scheduling database and EPS structure, connected by logical links, and opened as one schedule.

To achieve full schedule integration required in schedule quantification, the risk analyst has no better means but to use logical hard links between relevant project activities. It is the only effective way to ensure that calculation of critical path in the schedule remains possible and reliable.

Project managers have to find a method of doing away with the time-consuming collection of data from many fronts by offering a common database of information and the same scheduling environment to their contractors and clients. This is the best practice in coming up with "what you see is what you get" quality.

Without established relationships crossing individual and separated project schedules or work scopes, what could have been a fast and accurate identification of critical works becomes manual, tedious, and lengthy if not impossible.

We also have to remind ourselves that having another scope somewhere in another schedule is time-consuming, confusing, introduces inaccuracies, and is comparable to using another application. Such situation can easily lead to the managing overall schedule with two versions of the truth.

As there are no direct links between projects and sub-projects, it is most likely that each one has a different data date due to a different update cycle.

Know that all projects and sub-projects must have the same data date before calculating the schedule (F9) to derive critical paths and floats. The bigger the difference between data dates, the higher the chance of errors and inaccuracies!

If a project person will only think a little deeply about it, it can be very difficult and sometimes overwhelming, a counter-productive approach and a dangerous position to be in.

20. Schedule Risk Model

20-1   Very High-Level Summary (VHLS)

Back in 2009, a fellow AACE member demonstrated his preferred way of risk modeling. He asked the project team to prepare a model of the whole schedule, but with no more than 25 activities.

The thought of simplifying a multi-billion-dollar project that way brought a quick frown to some of us. It seems illogical and naïve, so we were quick to push back.

I, for one, implored him, "Good risk management relies on the presence of details. There must be enough details to make a good model which can lead to the best decision. If I am to convert a large schedule of, say 20,000 activities into 25 representative activities, will that be a good representation? I don't think so!" As he was not able to answer the question confidently in the affirmative, I felt that he was wasting time.

He tried to explain that the focus is to look only for those critical activities driving the completion date. The targets are those that fall along the primary and secondary critical paths, plus those activities not necessarily on the critical path but tagged as high schedule risks.

Another reason he offered as to why having a small number of summary activities is preferable is to minimize the effect of the Central Limit Theorem (CLT).

It is simpler and ensures a more productive workshop

59

process. The method will not require importing from the scheduling tool (e.g. Primavera or MS Project) into a risk assessment tool such as OPRA.

This suggested simplified method puts an end to the capacious risk models that beginners to the industry employ. It is expected to isolate the real points of concern from the noise by creating a simple and very high-level summary (VHLS) schedule risk model (Reference: Aug-2009, Iron Triangle Analysis (Methods and Concept) Discussion Thread Started and Facilitated by Rufran C. Frago, look for full commentary made by other participants).

20-2   Medium Level Summary

A schedule risk Medium Level Summary (MLS) model of major projects is one that consists of about 100 to 300 sensible medium level activities. This model makes more sense than a VHLS. MLS activities represent the overall project schedules longest path/critical, near critical and high-risk activities. I have applied the criteria to a Level 3 schedule where the count of remaining normal activities is greater than 3000.

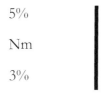

5%

Nm

3%

Where:

Nm is the number of remaining normal activities in the model. For more detailed schedule, Nm becomes Nd. Nd is the number of remaining normal activities in the detailed schedule.

A good number of risk analysts in the construction industry have expressed their preference for using a separate and summarized schedule model, compared to the use of the detailed and overly complex schedule.

They believe that they achieve a better and more acceptable result. It takes more time, but the separate model will also permit the risk analyst to advance his overall understanding of how the project schedule is established.

The identification of very few activities using the static primary and secondary critical path only, will not fly.

It seems like a good idea at first to newcomers, but as soon as one understands that static critical paths are not reliable, then it will not be so appealing.

 The critical path is dynamic and will probably change path as soon as the project updates the schedule. Apart from some activities with high criticality, the path is constantly changing.

What the scheduler filters from the schedule and what many, initially perceive as critical are just static paths, which are practically just snapshots of moments in time. This is only equivalent to one of the 1000 or more iterations carried out by OPRA (previously Pertmaster) or any of the other risk modeling tools available.

20-3   Fit for Purpose Model

We start with the objectives, followed by the methods. The process, although independent of the tool, should govern the use of the tool.

The modeling method should be "fit for purpose." In view of that, there can really be no standard way of doing it. The best anyone can do is to have some guidelines in place, then pick the best approach that satisfies the project's goals. It means that each project will have to come up with a unique set of criteria.

Since one of the fundamental and glaring attributes of a project is being a unique endeavor, fit-for-purpose approach makes the most sense. Unfortunately, that line of thinking puts into question the need for project benchmarks.

If one thinks about a new project relying heavily on benchmarked information of similar projects executed during the past years, there is a good chance that doing so might become the organization's pitfall. Why would it be?

 It can happen because of the basic premise that each project is unique. By logic, they might not be comparable.

Many organizations use benchmarks more often, i.e. clients and contractors alike, as an excuse not to conduct a full-blown quantitative risk analysis.

Using benchmark instead of going into risk quantification specific to the current project is common.

The project gravitates towards the tabulated results of their in-house or third-party consultant database even without understanding the attributes of each benchmark.

Are there built in risks in the benchmark? Is the benchmark applicable for use in North America? …in North Africa? …in Singapore? What assumptions were considered in this benchmark? Was this benchmark normalized? How was it normalized? What factors were taken out?

I have seen a few projects using such approach confused and derailed for leaning too much on the repeatability idea of project execution.

Using benchmark information without knowing their detailed attributes introduces unwelcome surprises. The information is a line on the sand that serves as reference. The unfortunate truth however, is that a project by its unique attributes, is not repeatable. In most instances, it does remain a line on the sand. In this sense, a benchmark is not a target.

One of the accepted online definitions of repeatability is the ability of an operator to repeat consistently the same measurement of the same part using the same gauge under the same conditions (Minitab, 2015). The ability to repeat is more operation in nature.

Are project management practitioners relying on a different degree of sameness and consistency as the definition of repeatability described by the aforementioned?

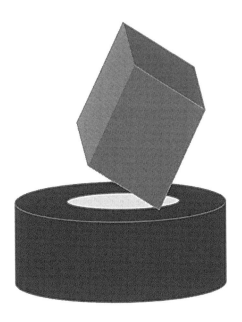 *General project practices can be repeatable but not the results. This kind of thinking, believing that a project can be repeatable to a degree like a manufacturing assembly line is easily the root cause of many project failures.*

Projects and operation differ primarily in that operations are ongoing and repetitive, while projects are temporary and unique (PMBOK® 6th Edition, 2019).

It is for the above reasons that I would recommend an integrated quantitative risk analysis for any substantially high-risk project.

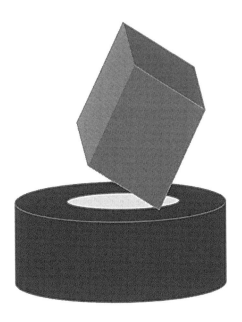

Figure 12 - Fit for Purpose Approach

20-4   Summary Model

Other analysts opined that summarizing the schedule is building a completely different schedule. It is quite doubtful that a junior or intermediate planner/scheduler could successfully do it.

It takes years of experience in the science of planning and scheduling before one can do so.

Inexperience can unintentionally bring into the summarized project schedule the following: transfer errors, omissions, flawed relationships, personal biases, and other issues.

The summarized schedule can end up completely departing from the details.

Think about this: if VHLS is the kind of simplification that we want to do, I can merely select any 15 to 30 activities.

I need not bother filtering the critical activities, because they might not be critical any more after the first schedule update.

As such, a 15 to 25-activity summary of a multi-billion-dollar mega-project will not be sufficient. This is a "very high-level summary" (VHLS) and can make many risk managers a bit uncomfortable. I disagree with the notion of creating a too simplistic schedule risk model.

 Risk management hinges very closely on enough details to be effective, and a VHLS does not provide enough.

If a straight-thinking person were to decide which schedule risk-model to use, VHLS will be out the window.

Even if you use one hundred (100) task summary schedule to model a huge project level 3 ten thousand (10,000) control schedule it won't work properly.

It would be like appreciating the whole universe by looking at earth's solar system alone or as one of my colleagues in a LinkedIn discussion thread puts it, "appreciating an original great work of art using a copy placed on a postage stamp."

21. VHLS Proponents

In fairness to the proponents of the VHLS methodology, I did ask a few of them to explain their rationale. The main reason given is obvious. They simply need to reduce a very large schedule to a more manageable size that can be analyzed within a reasonable time.

Proponent #1 replied:

"I take the whole project schedule and make sure it is up to date. Calculate the schedule to identify the critical paths (CP). Note that CP depends on how the project has defined it. Retain only the primary critical paths and those that the project believes are high risks work packages. After this is done, I ask the scheduler to delete everything else that falls outside the set criteria."

Proponent #2 replied:

"Using the VHLS method in SQRA is preferable if the quality of the overall schedule is not good. Take for example a big schedule of 10,000+ activities with a bunch of open-ends and dangling activities. These are indications of missing scopes and wrong logic ties. In my honest opinion, it is much better to build a representative summary schedule that reflects the real execution strategy and sequence. I want a model having the correct logic that will permit the unhampered, unconstrained flow of the schedule."

Proponent #3 replied:

"My consideration of the VHLS revolves around the

availability of time. I ask the project manager whether there is enough time to do the risk analysis. It is apparent that a summary schedule will take a smaller amount of time and simplify the model. Going through the facilitation process will be a breeze."

Proponent #4 replied:

"One of my friends in the risk management profession related that he has performed SQRA using the summary schedule approach, while their contractor performed a schedule risk using the detailed schedule. The results were similar and comparable. The difference was that the contractors work required over three weeks involving more than two subject matter experts to facilitate while the summary approach only took a week and one person."

Many project managers say that summarizing the schedule is not that hard. Proponents #1 to #3 and especially Proponent #4 have suggested it.

Re-creating a schedule through a representative summary requires someone with very strong planning, scheduling, and risk modeling knowledge and skills.

He should be able to visualize the overall execution strategy and capture it. It is reaching the main objective by traversing above the details, through the timeline on a zip line. Recreating a schedule cannot be overly simplistic or else we end up kidding ourselves.

Facilitating the 3-point estimate risk session using a summary schedule will be quite challenging. The disciplines might end up losing their independence, expertise, and confidence because the summary becomes too general.

22. Stop using VHLS?

Should mega-projects stay away from VHLS risk modeling? The method advocated by some consultants who believe it is possible to reduce a large control schedule of 10,000 activities to 100 (1% of the population) makes me frown. Do they really think that they can provide meaningful information to the project team? Do you believe that they can help find the correct schedule drivers and reduce schedule risk? It's doubtful!

It is advisable to support a summary schedule that offers enough meat for risk assessment but not a VHLS. The risk analyst must strike a balance when doing summary risk-model. He must find that sweet spot.

Some of us have done summary schedules on occasions in the past and they seem to work fine. Are we just lucky or did we hit that sweet spot regarding level of details?

As one matures in the risk management profession, it is prudent to stay away from oversimplifications, such as the creation of an equivalent VHLS risk model from a very detailed schedule like a Level 4 or Level 5.

Did you not notice that more information gets lost as the distance between each summary level increases? Try creating a level 1 schedule from a level 5 construction schedule. It is like reflecting an 8000-activity schedule into a one-activity schedule.

Does that make sense? Will it be useful as a schedule risk model? With all due respect to those who favor the very high-level summary version of a schedule as the risk quantification model, here are some of the reasons why I cannot embrace the method completely.

One must remember that summaries are high-level representation of the details. The higher the level, the harder it is to have acceptable logical links between activities in a schedule.

In such situations, a scheduling person uses more SS and FF scheduling relationships that rely heavily on lags and constraints. This decreases the quality of the schedule immensely. Excessive use of these SS, FF, and lags introduces inherent risks, while the constraints add unfounded certainty that welcomes error into the model.

 Summary schedule tends to rely heavily on constraints and lags. This is not desirable. Lags behave like normal but hidden activities.

This is not saying that the detailed schedule does not have its share of lags. The difference to consider here is the magnitude of the lags involved and the quality of the schedule. When this happens, we encounter the problem that it is better for some of lags to be visible, expressed as normal activities.

Take note that Primavera (P6) and OPRA consider the lag calendar in the calculation. The impact to the schedule or the risk model, depending on the tool's setting, will be immense.

The risk analyst who goes through the quantification

process blindly and remains unaware of the setup will have a problem because the imported dates will change and disagree with the detailed schedule.

 In several forums, I have always conveyed this rule of thumb: "The higher the level of the schedule, the greater the number of unknowns."

"And why is that?" you will ask.

The answer is simple. If we fly above a forest, we would not know exactly what is happening under the trees. Effective risk management requires details, and a VHLS certainly does not have enough.

The project manager will look at the schedule only to ask what is in there, only to realize there are several unknowns. Unless the manager knows the project's strategic objective, it will be difficult to connect the dots and decide.

If there is no unknown in the schedule, breaking it down is not necessary. If the schedule does not offer the details we want, we must break it down to smaller pieces.

The details are there so that we can clearly see the critical bumps and potholes. Look for the schedule drivers that the project needs to address along the path of travel. This will help ensure that we get to our destination on time, on quality, and on budget. Maybe we should be utilizing them, not hiding them.

We have to strike an acceptable balance.

23. Contracts & Schedules

How are contracts and level of schedule related? One factor to consider is the standard level of schedule required by the contract. It can be any level that the contract specifies.

Regardless of how much information the project has, if the contract says that it must be a level 3 control schedule, then it has to be a level 3. Other than the baseline, the control schedule is the schedule that is typically subjected to risk analysis. Even if the activity data is suitable for a lower level schedule such as level 4 or 5, the responsible party must prepare a level 3.

You must be ready to utilize whatever schedule is agreed-to by all contracting parties. If you are to risk analyze an approved baseline or control schedule that has 10,000 activities or more, you can proceed as is. Create the schedule risk-model from what is in front of you.

The number does not really matter, because all ranged values, correlations, and risk factors inputted into the select activities will always be part of the iteration. By proceeding to identify 500 long duration, critical, and near-critical activities to range belonging to the multiple critical paths, you have with all practicality able to focus on a reliable summary representation of the original schedule.

 SQRA iterates the risk-model considering the whole schedule.

It calculates various combinations of ranged values given

to 500 activities. A thousand iteration means you are looking at 1000 different project situations, or 1000 what-ifs. It follows then that five thousand iterations mean you are viewing 5000 project scenarios.

When one picks the critical and near critical activities from the original deterministic schedule, those activities belong to the static critical path. Once iteration starts, some of those activities will move away from the critical path and new critical activities will take their place.

You will identify areas of concern by tapping into the judgment of subject matter experts and third-party project management professionals. The risk register can offer additional information. You have the option to review the ranged values of the 500 activities.

Revalidate them with the the original source of information when the results do not make sense. Such review is acceptable. Just be careful that you do not fall into the trap of making adjustments to tailor the results.

The owner of the schedule should be the one to clean the schedule, nobody else. This includes fixing broken links, correcting logics, changing descriptions, or any modification and simplification. Schedule update is done by the responsible person, properly assigned, and designated to do the task.

Multiple Users modifying schedule attributes without any rule of engagement must be avoided. To go ahead haphazardly is to be sorry in the end.

The repercussions of touching and summarizing a schedule can be distressing. The peril of doing so without an agreed-to procedure is that as soon as the risk analyst touches, summarizes, and changes the schedule, the owner of the schedule, be it the client or the contractor, is already poised to disown it.

If that summarized schedule finally ever becomes the basis of the SQRA result, issues, disputes, and disagreements will likely occur between contracting parties. If that happens, relationship landscapes will not look good.

24. Optimum Size

What should really be the optimum size of the schedule model for risk analysis? Should it really be 150 to 300 activities? 500? 800? 1000? 2000? 3000? The final sample number shall depend on the total population of normal activities.

The discussion brings us back to the quality of the detailed schedule.

One must understand that if the project schedule is incompetently developed, the summary model or any smaller size representative risk model also suffers.

Even if it is not a VHLS, a good summary representation of the detailed schedule will depend greatly on its quality.

The danger for many beginners is that they too often tie themselves to the tools and applications without understanding the risk-based management processes involved.

You must not imprison your analytical work inside OPRA. Maintain that professional risk-based perspective broad in order not to fall prey to the dreaded enemy called familiarity, and monotony. The issue of risk analysts and schedulers as computer jockeys are well known.

 Take this advice from an old mentor, "The right division of knowledge is 80% process and 20% tools."

Do not be "Tool-centric" but be more "Process-centric." You decide whether this statement relates directly to the subject at hand.

Who knows? You might change your perspective. It's your decision how you create a balance.

25. Detailed Schedule

Running SQRA using the detailed schedule are becoming more practical than ever before despite claims by several experts that summary modeling works better and easier to understand.

OPRA as a risk analysis tool has no limitation to what it can handle. Running a project portfolio as large as 15,000 to 50,000 activities is not a problem. As to the accuracy and practicality of running such a large model, it can be as simple as one plus one or it can be quite complex. Ask yourself the following to help you decide.

- Completeness: Is the schedule complete? Does it have the entire scope?
- Accuracy: Did the model accurately reflect the execution plan? Do we have the same data date for all sub-projects?
- Timeliness: Do we have time to do a comprehensive SQRA?
- Fairness: Have we successfully removed input biases?
- Enforceability: Did the stakeholders approve this same schedule for SQRA?
- Methodology: Did we follow the standards and procedures governing this SQRA?
- Inherent risks: Were there any inherent risks identified?
- Project buy-in: Did the project accept the schedule constraints and assumptions?

26. ICSQRA

I strongly agree with a growing number of risk managers that the ideal method is an integrated cost and schedule quantitative risk analysis (ICSQRA).

Medium size to mega-projects should strive to unite these two components to get the complete picture. Doing them separately creates informational gaps.

One thing that an excellent risk practitioner should remember is not to rely on just one risk model. A singular risk model limits the project from seeing the best alternatives and courses of action.

Using two or more, or even several models give the project a better view of the situation and provides them with enough information to make the best decision.

Observing the behavior of other risk practitioners, I shake my head whenever one uses a singular model to come up with the results.

Running just one risk-model is a form of indolence and complacency. It needs to change to appreciate all facets of what could be.

It is best to run the process several times while varying certain input information, risk factors, and assumptions.

Tweaking and adjusting the risk schedule model

considering other factors will help generate all possibilities. Anything that makes good sense can be part of the equation.

If you think you missed anything, go back and run another simulation.

27. Political Dates

When a project presents a schedule model for SQRA, the schedule is the deterministic schedule from which all analysis emanates. The deterministic term is quite clear. It should not confuse anybody.

A deterministic schedule is a snapshot in time. The deterministic dates, including the end of the project date, become the point of reference to which schedule contingency is measured.

The risk analysis tool will allow the iteration to proceed with a simple warning regarding the relative values I mentioned. However, it will flag an error if the MAX value is less than the ML value, the ML value is greater than the MAX, or the MIN is greater than the ML.

The analyst must exercise care in accepting values from the stakeholders/participants without understanding the frame of mind from where they came from. It is important to bring everyone to think within one frame of thought so that all perspectives are from the same footing. It prevents selective perception.

 Selective perception refers to instances where you see what you want to see (Intaver, 2006). This occurs when one's intention is to fit or influence the estimate to fit the mandated cost limitation when preparing the project's budget.

It is also a well-known reason why projects force their schedule to satisfy mandated political dates. Many project managers will force-fit cost and schedule without blinking an eye or a pushback.

Then the problem starts.

Figure 13 – Political Dates

 Political dates are influencing factors to consider. It is the risk practitioner's responsibility to provide the facts of the matter. If the assessment is not positive, a responsible person should be honest about it.

A risk analyst worth his salt should be able to say with firm conviction that an optimistic or a pessimistic schedule is not an effective schedule.

What will you do if the management's target finish-date conflicts with what the developed project schedule reasonably shows?

If the Client company has mandated that the project should finish by June 1, 2018 and the most up to date deterministic schedule is showing July 25, 2018 instead, then a political date challenge is now in motion.

The project team knows that the updated control schedule can no longer reasonably achieve this date.

The schedule has negative float taken against the mandated date. The project schedule is forecasted to be delayed at the get-go. Everyone knows this even without doing an SQRA.

If after undergoing a thorough team review, and schedule adjustments reflecting the most likely scenario trying to meet the date but still to no avail. It ended with a date of July 25, 2018.

Let us say the project team exhausted all efforts and the overall schedule still ended with a deterministic date of July 25, 2018. What do you think should be the project's next course of action?

I guess you do not have to wait that long. The project manager asked you to do the schedule risk assessment.

You asked yourself, "What?! Do a risk analysis on an already delayed schedule? Would there even be value doing so? It is no longer a question of possible delay. It is already determined to be delayed."

28. Which model to use?

At once, the question you probably ask yourself is this: Which schedule should I use? Should I use the one with the management deterministic date of June 1, 2018 or the most likely schedule with a July 25, 2018 end date?

You were thinking that if you do the former, you need to crash and accelerate the schedule such that the last milestone falls on June 1, 2018. If you do the latter, no adjustment is needed on the available most-likely schedule.

In view of this management mandate, how should the project manager and his risk manager/analyst approach the SQRA process? What is the acceptable schedule risk-model to this political date apparent dilemma?

The answer is simple. The analyst can opt to use anyone of the two risk-models. First option is to use the June 1, 2018 management date as is. It is considered the target date while July 25, 2018 remains the deterministic date. This option is better than the second one as it does not involve changing the most likely deterministic schedule.

The schedule is left alone to reflect the most likely end date as per approved execution plan (i.e. the plan is not massaged to fit the management date!).

Risk analysis shall report the probability of achieving both, the target and the deterministic dates. The second option is to accelerate the schedule. Adjust and shorten the activities lying on the static critical path. Reviewing delivery cycle, and work methodology can open good opportunities.

Add to the exercise efficient scope management, value engineering, and effective resource assignments, all with the intent of pulling in the end deliverable and finally achieving the management date objective. The rationale is that the project management must know the probability of achieving both the target and deterministic dates.

What that project team chooses to report to its client, sponsors, and board is a team decision. The final SQRA results will help in that decision.

Now, let me ask you this. If June 1, 2018 is the target date and July 25, 2018 is the deterministic date, then what is the calculated schedule contingency? What is the best and proper way of reflecting contingency on the distribution chart?

In this situation, we encounter the term "target date." Do you believe that it is an acceptable SQRA term? How would you reflect this management target date on the generated distribution chart? How are you going to report its relevance to the calculation of schedule contingency?

I tried looking for guidance in the early years of my career as a risk management practitioner but was not able to find a solid answer. As the years went by, the answer presented itself. I found that having a target date is not really a big deal. It is practically but a question of proper communication, buy-in, and approval.

The probabilities of all focused dates are all easily extractable. If the management target date prevailed over the deterministic end date, then schedule contingency shall refer to that date.

The apparent difficulty lies in the basic premise that

schedule contingency is the difference between the project's risk probability standard which is the P50 in this example, and the deterministic date.

Since the client has mandated the project should finish on June 1, 2018 and the most likely deterministic schedule ends on July 25, 2018, the contingency cannot be determined based on this formula. Schedule contingency shall be the difference between the standard P-date and the management target date.

Using **Figure 14** distribution chart, the calculated contingency is equal to August 5, 2018 (P50) minus June 1, 2018 (Target Date), a difference of 65 days or nine (9) weeks.

One must take note that the target date of June 1, 2018 has zero probability. While this is so, it is not a far cry from the most likely deterministic schedules of less than P1.

If you chose the second option as your schedule risk model, the deterministic end date is equal to the management target date. The calculation of P50 minus Pd (Deterministic) is more straight-forward. In this model, the schedule contingency is P50 minus <P1 (deterministic), resulting in 11 days or ~1.5 weeks.

If the project risk appetite (risk standard) is P70 and not P50, then the resulting schedule contingency is equal to P70 date of August 8, 2018 minus <P1 deterministic date of July 25, 2018, calculated to 14 days or 2 weeks.

Through this, the project can be objective in laying out its case strongly to the leaders.

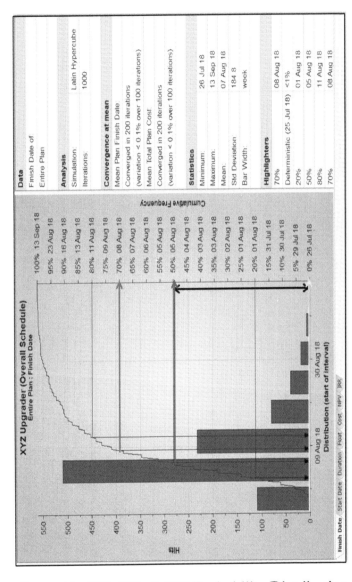

Figure 14 - P10, P50, & P70 Probability Distribution

29.SQRA Preparation

It is like painting a wall. The wall preparation takes the longest before the final paint coat is applied. The last coat becomes as important as sanding debris and covering all holes with joint compound.

Up to 80 percent of the effort in Schedule Quantitative Risk Analysis (SQRA) is spent in the preparation of the risk model. The remaining twenty percent (20%) is spent on the proper use of OPRA.

 If the model was not properly represented in OPRA, then the 80% effort amounted to nothing. The assessment result will be unreliable if not wrong. It is a mortal sin to the analyst! This can derail a project!

SQRA basic preparation includes the following:

1. Identification of the right stakeholders and resources who will provide the duration ranges and critical risk inputs.
2. Arrangement of effective risk workshops. Choosing the proper venue sets the tone of a serious, goal-oriented workshop. Risk facilitators must not take the workshop for granted
3. Holding one-on-one or group interviews.
4. Ensuring that the risk model was derived from a good quality schedule.
5. Proper use of the risk analysis tool.
6. Relevant driving planning documents must be ready as references about three (3) to four (4) weeks before quantitative risk analysis workshop. These are critical

documents that will provide necessary information in formulating a dependable result.

- List of schedule's key and critical milestones.
- Participative planning minutes of meeting and attendance sheet, including action plans. These documents ensure that all schedule stakeholders were involved in the planning process and support the developed schedule.
- Input sheet, also called risk interview worksheet (see **Figure 15**). This typical worksheet designed for traditional duration ranging and risk analysis review helps a lot. It provides an outstanding perspective on why the subject matter expert (SME) and/or stakeholders provided the 3-point estimate values they have given. The table contains the recorded three-point inputs of the discipline subject matter experts on individual activity and relevant work packages. It gives perspective as to why experts (interviewees) gave the values they have given. A note column on this same sheet must explain in brief what risk were considered if there was one. If it is because of pure estimating uncertainty, the column field corresponding to the activity can remain blank.
- A native file of the schedule. If the application used is Primavera P6, then the XER or XML (both Primavera native files) of the deterministic schedule is preferred transmitted via e-mail over a file located in a common database or folder.

This file contains the schedule for risk analysis. Submission is best coursed through an official e-mail to document the official transmittal. This becomes more important when dealing with joint venture partners, vendors, consultants, contractors, and subcontractors.

By getting the XER, MPP, or PLAN files conveyed officially, the subject schedule sample is practically unchanged.

If any dispute comes up as to the validity of the original sample, the transmittal document will be the deciding factor.

In this way, there will be no confusion as to what file will be analyzed. The file sent through e-mail is an official submission.

 It is important for the project team to have reviewed the submitted deterministic sample schedule, and giving their buy-in before any schedule risk quantification starts.

- An approved Basis of Schedule or BOS (Schedule Basis & Methodology).

  The BOS holds collated data from where the schedule bases its information. It has key milestone dates, work breakdown structure hierarchy, coding keys, calendar bases, resource bases, etc.

  The project submits the BOS first, before the schedule corresponding thereto.

- A schedule quality check report based on your

company's or project's established Minimum Schedule Quality (MSQ). If these are not yet available in your organization as benchmarks, then it is about time to create one.

- Approved Estimate Summary

- Approved Basis of Estimate
- Approved Detailed Estimate

- Latest and updated Risk Register

- Approved and updated Project Charter

- Latest and updated Project Execution Plan

- Project Kick-off Presentation

- Latest Project Monthly Report

- Assumption Log and Constraint Log

The responsible project risk manager must ensure that the schedule quantitative risk analysis process follows the governing standards and procedures of the project organization. A change management notice or deviation notice covers any substantial deviation from the standard approaches. This is essential in managing change and holds much value when evaluating the subsequent results. It is also an important record during future schedule benchmarking initiatives.

Many in the engineering and construction industry think that the tool is but a push of a button and there's not much intelligent thought or skills needed to come up with a result.

Managers typically have a strong bias against tool experts, short of calling them tool-centric ignoramus who do not really know what risk-based management process is about. It is funny that despite that perception, they do call these experts every time.

This self-defeating perspective makes project managers miss out. They will come out of the engagement without anything of value.

The truth is, risk-based processes are as important as the tool. The tool is the vehicle that carries the process into completion.

Your inability to operate the tool the right way will ultimately fail the process. You must use the tool to the tool right!

It will render all the preparation, data gathering techniques, and in-depth project discussions, regardless of how conscientious it was done, inadequate or useless!

Performing a Monte Carlo or a Latin Hypercube simulation is the core of SQRA in OPRA.

Going through the motion of quantification from importing to report generation without understanding how tool settings and flawed data translation affect the result is very common.

In my profession, I have reviewed several risk analysis results in my professional life that were disturbingly flawed because of how the analyst handled Primavera (P6) and OPRA. Wrong results and unwanted consequences give way wasted hours pursuing efforts that won't work.

Due to flawed risk assessment report, projects might try to start activities outside their ideal time frame, or embark on methodologies too difficult to execute if not impossible.

False critical paths generated might create unwarranted concerns, put all in panic mode, and confuse the planning and execution team putting out a fire that was not really there.

A schedule accepted for risk analysis that greatly deviates from the project execution plan creates troubling scenarios that keep project managers unreasonably on edge.

One must not forget the cardinal rule that the schedule is a reflection of the plan.

If the construction execution plan violates the overall strategy of execution, the project is good candidate for failure. Everyone should be on deck and looking at the same goal if it is to succeed.

When an analyst gets the sample of the schedule to be analyzed, it is his duty to make sure that the schedule quality meets the accepted criteria and best practice.

Go back and review Lesson 13 to sink it in.

Activity ID	Activity Name	Rem Dur	Start	Finish	Min Duration	Most Likely	Max Duration	Resources
Batangas Upgrader								
Detailed Engineering			19-Apr-10 A	29-Nov-10				
BATS-ENG001	Building Permit	15	29-Sep-10	21-Oct-10	15	15	20	
BATS-ENG003	Bid Clarifications - Well Manifold Module	6	15-Jul-10	26-Jul-10	6	6	6	
BATS-ENG004	RFP - Well Manifold Module	10	6-Aug-10	20-Aug-10	7	10	15	
BATS-ENG006	RFQ - VFD Building Module	10	3-Aug-10	17-Aug-10	6	10	15	
BATS-ENG007	TBE / RFP - VFD Building Module	10	15-Sep-10	29-Sep-10	6	10	15	
BATS-ENG009	P&ID IFC (Module)	10	24-Jun-10 A	23-Jul-10	10	10	10	
BATS-ENG010	LDT IFC (Module)	10	30-Jun-10 A	23-Jul-10	10	10	10	
BATS-ENG011	P&ID IFC (Off-Module)	8	26-Jul-10	6-Aug-10	8	8	13	
BATS-ENG012	LDT IFC (Off-Module)	8	26-Jul-10	6-Aug-10	8	8	13	
BATS-ENG013	Shutdown Key IFC	10	9-Aug-10	23-Aug-10	10	10	15	
BATS-ENG014	Control Philosphy IFC	10	16-Aug-10	30-Aug-10	10	10	15	
BATS-ENG016	CWP P&ID / Line List / Tie-in List	12	23-Aug-10	9-Sep-10	12	12	17	

Figure 15 - Interview Sheet

30.Engagement Process

In this section, we will touch on the step-by-step engagement that needs to happen leading to the final risk facilitation (duration ranging session), SQRA report generation, presentation, and interpretation of the results. In the course of the proceedings, much of the responsibility lies on the client's shoulder. This is because all the givens, the plans, estimates, bases, and working inputs come from or through them.

STEP 1

Client to submit essential supporting planning documents. Review of project execution plan documentation, e.g. Project summary information slides explaining background, path of construction, risk register (high risk), existing issues, problems, baseline/current schedule, constraints, and others as needed.

For normal small to medium size projects, it is ideal to submit all required input documents no later than three weeks before the risk quantification interactive session (three point ranging). The latest is 14 days before the facilitated session. For larger and/or more complex project, four weeks (4W) is suggested. These timelines can vary depending upon the analyst work load and expertise. It is designed to give the Risk Analyst enough time to review the materials and extract needed information most useful in schedule risk modeling.

STEP 2

Submit/transmit file (XER, XML or MPP) of the PROJECT SCHEDULE to be risk analyzed for quality assessment. Recommended practice requires that it represents the latest (one that is not more than two update cycles).

Include list of scheduling assumptions, constraints, and high risk issues, Basis of Schedule (BOS), Basis of Estimate (BOE), and Estimate Summary document.

It is important that the schedule has been reviewed by the project team/stakeholders and have their official buy-in. For normal small to medium size projects, it is ideal to submit all required input documents no later than two weeks before the risk quantification interactive session (three point ranging). The latest is seven (7) days before the facilitated session. These timelines can vary depending upon the analyst's work load and expertise.

STEP 3

Client has to provide the list of the top five (5) critical project milestones. This usually includes Construction Complete and Final Turnover when the overall schedule is fully integrated containing all phases. For example:

- TCCC LP Natural Gas
- Delivery Substation
- TCCC Vent Gas
- TCCC Electrical 4160V
- First Oil (FO)

Depending on how important each of the work packages are, other possible critical milestone candidates for monitoring and control are as follows; the client's project control team has to have good understanding of what milestones need closer look. The final list will also largely depend on the type of project and what industry this project belongs.

If you are the consultant or the risk analyst tasked in running the SQRA, you can make sound suggestions but in the end, the client has final say. Shown below are typical Oil and Gas Construction project milestones.

- Award PO Pipe Fabrication
- 1st Model Review - Tank Lot and Piperack
- Award PO Structural Steel
- 2nd Model Review - Piperack
- Issue P&ID IFC
- 1st Model Review - Process Area
- 2nd Model Review - Process Area
- Install Piling - NE Tank Farm
- Award PO Substation / EHouse 2&3
- Install Foundations - NE Tank Farm
- 3rd Model Review - Process Area
- Delivery (Hot Facility) Drain Tank
- Delivery of VCU Package
- Install Piling - Blended Bitumen Area
- Install Foundations - Blended Bitumen Area

For normal small to medium size projects, it is ideal to submit this milestone list at the get-go or no later than 7 days before the facilitated risk session. For larger and/or more complex project, two weeks (2W) is suggested. These timelines can vary depending upon the analyst/consultant's work load and expertise.

STEP 4

Identify client's in-house minimum schedule quality requirement if available. If not, use PM Solution Pro sixteen-point metrics (PMSP16) or anyone of the recommended schedule quality metrics offered by Acumen Fuse like DCMA 14.

You can also choose to create and customize your own or use anyone of the built in criterium.

If quality issues are found, the project is expected to address and improve them.

If the project decides to stick to the original unqualified schedule, the analyst must assertively push back.

If the client insists, risk analyst can proceed with a caveat. The client representative must understand that the project will then have to shoulder any inherent risks associated with the unreliable results.

The findings must be included in the project risk register as an official red flag.

For normal small to medium size projects, it is ideal to identify the in-house schedule quality criteria of the client. The analyst shall ensure that there is agreement as to the minimum quality required upon submission of the schedule's native file.

All quality issues must be resolved no later than five (5) to six (6) days before the facilitated risk session. For larger and/or more complex project, seven (7) days to ten (10) days is suggested. This timeline can vary depending upon the analyst/consultant's work load and expertise.

STEP 5

Consultant shall develop schedule risk models based on agreed approaches. In this book, we will use the traditional, multiple CPM approach.

It is very important to identify client's standard risk appetite (risk threshold). You will refer to it when calculating your schedule contingency.

31. Required Participants

Project stakeholders or their duly designated representatives (delegates) are the best participants. They have the authority to give inputs on behalf of the group they belong to or represent.

They are there to answer whatever clarifying question might come up during the SQRA facilitated process. Stakeholders who have the power to decide and influence matters within the confine of their individual expertise are invited.

Some facilitators try to avoid inviting managers and directors to the session because the perception is that they end up babying the project, mixing bias into their inputs. This might not at all be true always but being aware of this concern can help you govern the process better.

Front-end specialists and experts often come up with excellent objective feedback.

If management participates, it is more to balance overall perspective, help facilitate collaboration, provide relevant management information, and encourage free speech among the front-end leaders and disciplines.

It is suggested that the planner/scheduler, senior risk specialist, and risk manager facilitate the session.

They should develop a strategy on how to extract the best information.

Recommended list of stakeholders and project team

members (but not limited to) who must provide the needed risk inputs. Here are some of them:

- Engineering Leads
- Procurement Leads
- Contracting Leads
- Project Controls Specialists
- Lead Estimator
- Planning/Scheduling Specialists
- Construction Supervisor/Foremen
- Modularization Supervisor/Foremen
- Fabrication Supervisor/Foremen
- Senior Risk Specialist (can help facilitate)
- Risk Manager (can help facilitate)
- Project Manager
- Engineering Manager
- Project Controls Manager
- Risk Manager
- Environmental, Health, and Safety Manager
- Operation representative
- Essential others

That last item "Essential others" refers to any additional and relevant project personnel who can provide valuable input on risks associated with and/or affecting the schedule; e.g. regulatory specialists, camp coordinators, contractor representative, union representatives, progress specialists, commissioning and start up leads, and so on.

Whoever can fill that existing information gap is a potential invitee.

32. Modeling Philosophy

The list below enumerates the more common OPRA importing issues. Together, we will look at them individually and identify the solution. Knowing how to fix them, will provide you a feeling of confidence and independence. You will encounter these challenges in the future. Be glad that you have it all figured out today!

The risk analyst or person facilitating the risk session has the responsibility to help all participating disciplines, stakeholders, and subject matter experts adjust their thinking according to a common approach.

This is not to influence the perspective or assessment of individual participants. It is to keep the thinking process within acceptable bounds.

The participants must observe the recommendations of the risk analyst. This is to prevent the inputs from going so far outside the acceptable sample norms that they become skewed or biased.

The schedule is fast-tracked. This does not mean fast-tracking an already delayed schedule but merely describing the best practice economical method of scheduling using parallel execution of activities. Use fast-tracking whenever reasonable and achievable.

The schedule model shall closely follow the following

guiding principles:

- As much as possible, there must be no built-in risk in the schedule. Risk brought about by complexity or contracts difficult to implement are not to be considered as part of the baseline model. They have to be captured in the risk register and considered during the risk analysis session as influencing factors in the calculation of contingency.
- Alignment to implementation plan and execution strategy.
- The schedule duration is based on high performance teams (qualified team members).

  Here's a philosophical question you might ask. How would one know that they have highly qualified team members? Each team member would think that they are highly qualified or they would not be part of the team!

  The statement is but a theoretical scenario that an analyst must contemplate on a little deeper and later on consider during the course of risk assessment. If the risk facilitator is smart, he will quickly discern the true colors of the participants and make adjustments accordingly.

- Schedule details are in accordance with the project stage.
- The schedule aligns to the current frozen estimate.
- Schedule duration represent modal (most likely), median (P50 midpoint), or mean (average)

values.

- Assume no restrictions on E, P, M, C, or C&SU resources.
- Ranged values did not result from double dipping; e.g. risked quantities that are already quantified in the project risk register.

33. Guide to Ranging

As mentioned in the previous section, provide a clear guide to the participants formulating the ranges. A realistic boundary needs to be set in order to avoid too much optimism or pessimism. This is to avoid extremely skewed overall results. Ensure accurate modeling to prevent this from happening.

The list below will help.

Optimistic durations
- Participant's best experience in the last 10 years, or the last 10 projects (1 in 10 scenarios)

Most likely durations
- Participant's average experience in the last 10 years, or
- Based purely on the current estimate; i.e. it can represent modal or median values, whichever is available.

In statistics, the mode of a set of data values is that value appearing most often. "It is the value x at which its probability mass function takes its maximum value, the value that is ***most likely*** to be sampled (Wikipedia, Mode (statistics), 2019)".

Pessimistic durations
- Participant's worst experience in the last 10 years, or his last 10 projects (1 in 10 scenarios)

The most common distribution profile is triangular

(**Figure 16**). It is easier to understand the concept of a three-point range by picturing a triangle. The three vertices of the triangle represent Minimum Duration, Most Likely Duration, and Maximum Duration.

The empty space regions of the triangle are experiential void space of which the participant subject matter experts have no knowledge. SMEs might be able to interpolate these regions if given some additional external information.

Note that uncertainty and risk events are two components of the distribution. They are two main considerations in coming up with the duration values. Take, for example, an activity that will most likely take 10 days, plus or minus 2 days. The triangular duration range of 8, 10, and 12 days represents estimating uncertainties. The situation is normal, and no risk event is in play.

Now, let us reflect on this.

If a risk event has a high probability of occurring during the scheduled work, the SME can proceed to quantify the possible impact to an otherwise normal course of work that already has a small amount of uncertainty.

The potential late delivery of certain accessories can add some days to the pessimistic or maximum duration. Instead of 12 days, the participants can add or subtract a few days or weeks. He has to look for both positive and negative effects of risk; i.e. threats and opportunities.

There are a few ways to capture the effect of risks and uncertainties. The risk analyst has to have a good approach and an open mind. He has to listen closely to the participants so he will not miss anything of major importance from what they are saying.

What could be an opportunity might be mistakenly identified as a threat. If you are the risk analyst, you need to set the tempo and the direction to come up with the most reliable results.

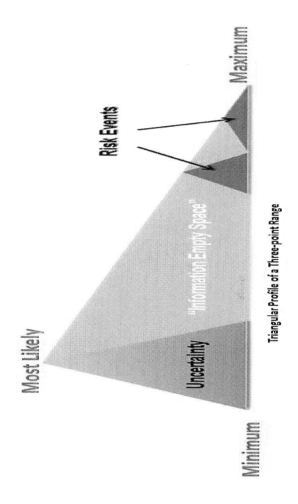

Figure 16 – Three-point Range

34. Avoid Double-dipping

Double dipping is a common problem in the traditional three-point estimating process involving risk events consideration.

The participating disciplines and stakeholders tend to come up with risk events already captured in the risk register.

The risk analyst should be constantly aware of this possibility.

The problem happens when risk events that were qualified and quantified using the risk register are now again part of the discussion in SQRA.

If they are not promptly flagged and identified, they become part of the quantification process despite having been considered, with impacts calculated previously and added to the total cost contingency while using the risk register.

They can drive the ranges once they become part of the calculation. This double-dipping scenario will create an unreliable end-result.

Only those risks not found in the risk register, or even if present in the risk register but not yet evaluated against the time component, are best included in the schedule risk analysis.

35. Common issues

The list below enumerates the more common OPRA importing issues.

Together, we will look at them individually and identify the solution.

Knowing how to fix them, will provide you a feeling of confidence and independence.

> **Issue-1:** Import start and finish dates in OPRA have unacceptable variances, as large as several days, sometimes weeks. The variances were easily confirmed with the original Primavera schedule file (source of the XER used in importing to OPRA).

> **Issue-2:** Translation of activity duration ranges when imported to OPRA was wrong. The optimistic, most likely, and pessimistic duration values were different from the source file.

> **Issue-3:** The primary critical path in OPRA was different from the critical path in P6 where the original source file came from.

Only through a meticulous, mathematical, and methodical process of risk modeling, a project manager will be able to identify, calculate, assess, and predict the following.

Otherwise, small pitfalls on the proper use of the OPRA tool are enough to render everything to naught.

By following certain recommended criteria governing schedule quality, the project can guard against wrong schedule risk assessment.

It is therefore expected that all project management practitioners understand the project's minimum schedule quality requirements.

A good manager who ignores or intentionally skips schedule quality check and quantitative risk analysis, loses many great opportunities to manage even better.

Regardless of the apparent challenges revolving around the subjectivity of the process, with right, logical, and intelligent inputs, SQRA will give the project a sound basis when making a difficult choice.

It will provide a solid foundation when announcing a "Go or No Go" project decision.

36. Import Issues

An important major project schedule was recently imported to Oracle Primavera Risk Analysis for schedule quantitative risk analysis (SQRA).

The result of the import check revealed several large variances on the start and finish deterministic dates when compared to the original schedule (source).

The imported start and finish dates of 20 activities varies from the original deterministic dates by 5 days to as high as 33 days.

This is a common problem that got many self-professed risk subject matter experts scratching their heads. In many instances, the variances between the imported schedule and the source schedule were even bigger.

They can run from a month, two months, three months, or more.

There are schedule misalignments brought about by some differences in schedule configurations and individual activity attributes.

The simple requirement is for the schedule imported in OPRA to be the same as the source schedule.

If it comes from P6, then the P6 schedule must have the same attributes and values when viewed and displayed in OPRA.

The analyst must seek the highest level of alignment possible.

Most pervasive misalignment issues in terms of visibility are the following:

- Dates (Start and Finish)
- Durations

  - Remaining
  - Minimum
  - Most Likely
  - Maximum

- Critical path
- Calendars
- Calculation settings

  - Retained logic vs progress override
  - Lags (Successor vs predecessor)
  - Total Float vs Longest Path

- Data dates
- Constraints

  - Primary
  - Secondary

- Resources

The person who is responsible to pull together the schedule risk-model has that important responsibility to find the root cause of the problem and resolve it. He knows that the result of risk quantification will come out erroneous if the date misalignment stays.

The calculated probability, the schedule contingency, the forecast, the schedule drivers, and many other result elements will be wrong.

While handling schedules from different sources, the schedule risk analyst is bound to encounter numerous challenges putting an acceptable schedule risk-model together in OPRA. Problems that are not resolved become issues that can derail the timely completion of the analysis.

The correctness, accuracy, completeness, and usefulness of a Schedule Quantitative Risk Analysis (SQRA) will depend heavily on the quality of planning data used for input, or more plainly, the quality of the project schedule.

The quality of the source schedule (P6) and the imported schedule (OPRA) influence the quality of the analysis.

The rule is simple. All of us have heard it before. Garbage in, is garbage out or GIGO (Wikipedia, Garbage in, Garbage Out, 2013). It is an old rule of thumb, and one of the main reasons why an analyst needs to perform the qualitative process before the quantitative one.

Quality of system output depends on the quality of system input (Jill Butler, 2010).

It is a golden rule, one of the principal reasons as to why risk qualification comes before risk quantification.

Good inputs beget good outputs. The quality of working data is the foundation of a credible result. Organizations have to select acceptable schedule quality criteria to compare to.

This benchmark is a measuring stick of all deterministic schedules before they are risk analyzed.

A good quality schedule is a critical prerequisite for a successful quantitative exercise.

As we go forward to the tool-centric discussion of SQRA, we will have to check closely whether the schedule we have on our hands has the required minimum quality.

Being able to appreciate how and why certain schedule quality criteria are critical and important will ultimately govern how schedule risk models are prepared.

The relationship of SQRA and schedule quality is undeniable.

It is for this reason that the quality of schedule input can turn out to be the project's number one risk driver.

37. Review, Fix the Issues, and Run Simulations

Early on a Monday, one of the project's OPRA Users reported high variances between the imported dates and the original schedule dates from Primavera.

He did not have this problem before because he was using a singular calendar in his engineering schedules.

Now that the schedule has an integrated modularization, fabrication, field construction, and commissioning phase, he encountered misalignment issues on imported dates. Variances were big and unacceptable.

He murmured, "Must be the multiple calendars in the schedule that's causing it. It's the only attribute that has changed."

The User's evaluation of his issue was correct. He hit it right on the head.

Dates discrepancies is the result of translational variances created by OPRA during import. It changes certain attributes that it cannot firmly accept due to some source values and target configurations that were not fine-tuned or properly adjusted.

It is required that the original Primavera schedule equals OPRA's imported Schedule.

While the intention is to have them perfectly matching, the User ended up with two misaligned schedules.

To replicate the issue, I have created Project-A (Figure 17). This project has different calendars for each summary phase.

Each calendar has a different time period setting; i.e. working hours per day and working days per week.

It is an Engineering, Procurement, Modularization, Construction, & Start-up (EPMC/CSU) overall Schedule.

The following calendars were assigned to activities belonging to each phase.

A 5-2-8 Calendar for Engineering is a 5 day on, 2 days off Calendar @ 8 hours per day

A 5-2-10 Calendar for Module and Fabrication is a 5 day on, 2 days off Calendar @ 10 hours per day

A 10-4-10 Calendar for Construction is a 10 day on, 4 days off Calendar @ 10 hours per day

A 24/7 Calendar for Commissioning and Start-up is a 7 day on continuous @ 24 hours per day

Go to the original schedule in Primavera Project Management (P6) activity window.

Key in the *Optimistic, Most Likely*, and *Pessimistic* duration values using P6 User Defined Fields on selected activities (Figure 18 - P6 Activity View showing Durations & Duration Ranges).

In this simple example all activities were ranged. They were all assigned the three-point estimate.

Export the schedule XER file to an accessible project directory.

Open OPRA and import the XER from the project directory.

The imported schedule should include the three-point values in each selected activity.

To demonstrate the issues that the OPRA User was complaining about, the standard 8-hour per day time-period import setting was initially assigned (Figure 19).

This setting demonstrated that it will not work on a multi-calendar schedule.

Upon pressing OK, the import process commences.

The import will generate a log after each import is completed (Figure 20).

The User can then choose directory where to save it (Figure 21).

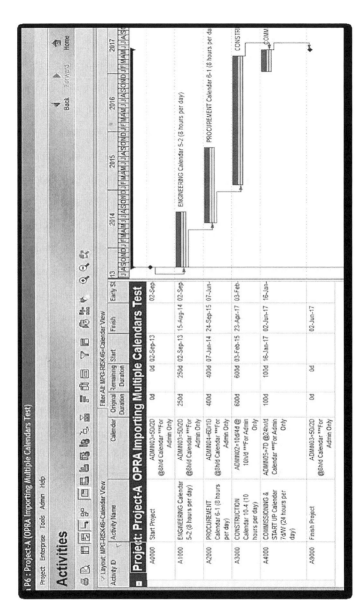

Figure 17 - Project A Activity View

126

P6 : Project-A (OPRA Importing Multiple Calendars Test)

Project Enterprise Tools Admin Help

Activities

Layout MPG-RISK46-Calendar View | Filter All: MPG-RISK46-Calendar View

Back Forward

Project: Project-A OPRA Importing Multiple Calendars Test

Activity ID	Activity Name	Calendar	Original Duration	Remaining Duration	Start	Finish	Early Start	Early Finish	Late Start	Late Finish	UDF Min Duration	UDF Most Likely	UDF Max Duration
A0000	Start Project	ADMIN03~5D/2D @8hd Calendar ***For Admin Only	0d	0d	02-Sep-13		02-Sep-13		02-Sep-13				
A1000	ENGINEERING Calendar 5-2 (8 hours per day)	ADMIN03~5D/2D @8hd Calendar ***For Admin Only	250d	250d	02-Sep-13	15-Aug-14	02-Sep-13	15-Aug-14	02-Sep-13	15-Aug-14	200	250	300
A2000	PROCUREMENT Calendar 6-1 (8 hours per day)	ADMIN04~6D/1D @8hd Calendar ***For Admin Only	400d	400d	07-Jun-14	24-Sep-15	07-Jun-14	24-Sep-15	07-Jun-14	24-Sep-15	300	400	500
A3000	CONSTRUCTION Calendar 10-4 (10 hours per day)	ADMIN02~10d/4d @10hd ***For Admin Only	600d	600d	03-Feb-15	23-Apr-17	03-Feb-15	23-Apr-17	03-Feb-15	23-Apr-17	500	600	800
A4000	COMMISSIONING & START UP Calendar 7dW (24 hours per day)	ADMIN05~7D @24hd Calendar ***For Admin Only	100d	100d	16-Jan-17	02-Jun-17	16-Jan-17	02-Jun-17	16-Jan-17	02-Jun-17	50	100	150
A9000	Finish Project	ADMIN03~5D/2D @8hd Calendar ***For Admin Only	0d	0d		02-Jun-17		02-Jun-17		02-Jun-17			

Figure 18 –P6 Activity View showing Ranges

127

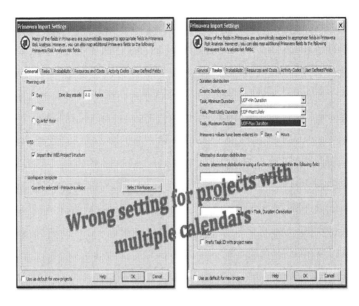

Figure 19 – OPRA Import Settings Window

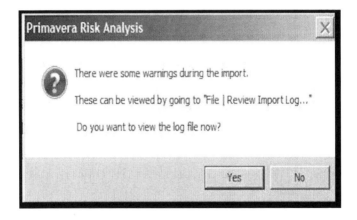

Figure 20 – OPRA Import Log Dialogue Box

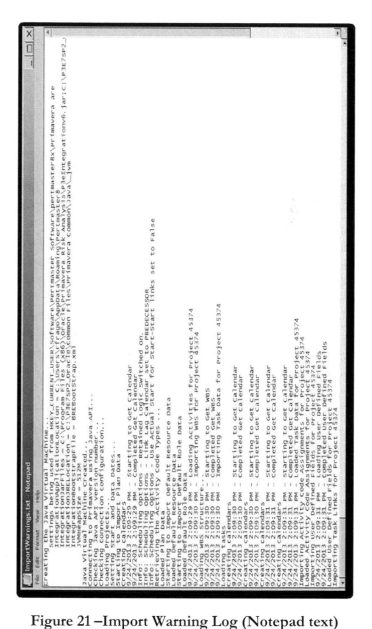

Figure 21 –Import Warning Log (Notepad text)

Lags and leads calculation with respect to the associated calendars contributed to the issue. The differences were too high and too many. As demonstrated in Figure 22 – Result of Import Check, the finish deterministic date of the project has moved to the right by 114 days. The standard 8-hour per day setting resulted in several unacceptable variances.

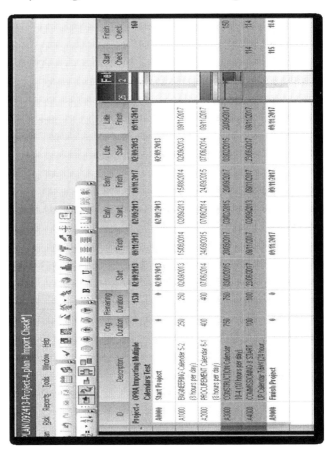

Figure 22 – Result of Import Check

Data quality of the schedule risk-model was poor,

making the results of SQRA in error. Import to OPRA of the original schedule produced wrong deterministic dates. The deterministic launching point dates were unreliable. It was also observed that some of the translated ranges were wrong. Activity A3000 for example showing 400, 480 & 640 (Figure 23- OPRA Activity View showing the Translated Min, ML & Max Duration). It should have shown 500, 600, and 800. Something is not right. The translation of the ranged values was in error.

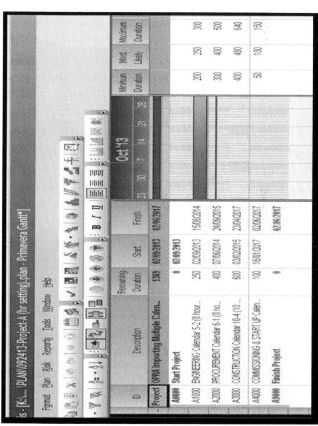

Figure 23 –Translated Min, ML & Max Duration

Importing a schedule with singular calendar to OPRA will not have the same issue. Translation of duration ranges is simple and straightforward. If the calendar "time period" is 8 hours per day for example, the import unit of conversion will be the same, i.e. 8 hours per day.

The large variances were due to improper import preparation of the original schedule, coupled with wrong settings in OPRA during import of multiple calendars schedule. An adjustment to the import setting is necessary.

The only way multiple calendar projects can be properly imported is to convert the durations of the ranges into hours using the right time-period setting of hours/day based on how the activities corresponding thereto was mapped to a specific calendar. You must change all the duration range values to hours to prepare them for import to OPRA.

Follow this explanation closely: An activity with a three-point range of 100 days, 150 days and 200 days minimum, most likely and maximum duration activity respectively, with a calendar time period of 10 hours per day will have to be converted to hours using the aforementioned time period value.

The converted three-point range for that activity is as follows:

100 days X 10 hours/day   =   1000 hours

150 days X 10 hours/day   =   1500 hours

200 days X 10 hours/day   =   2000 hours

A schedule segment of Project-A schedule (Figure 24 -

Project A Showing the Translated Min, ML, & Max Duration in Hours) shows the converted day's ranges to hours. The following illustration should provide a clear explaination.

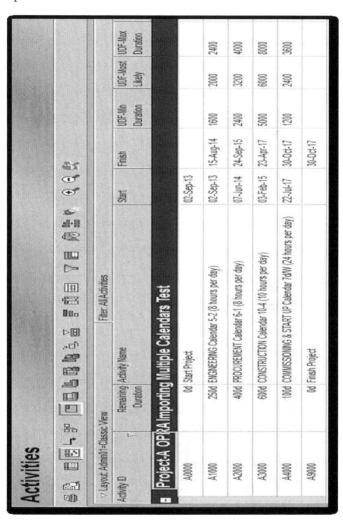

Activities

Layout: Admin01=Classic View   Filter: All Activities

Project-A OP&A Importing Multiple Calendars Test

Activity ID	Remaining Duration	Activity Name	Start	Finish	UDF-Min Duration	UDF-Most Likely	UDF-Max Duration
A0000	0d	Start Project	02-Sep-13				
A1000	25d	ENGINEERING Calendar 5-2 (8 hours per day)	02-Sep-13	15-Aug-14	1600	2000	2400
A2000	40d	PROCUREMENT Calendar 6-1 (8 hours per day)	07-Jun-14	24-Sep-15	2400	3200	4000
A3000	60d	CONSTRUCTION Calendar 10-4 (10 hours per day)	03-Feb-15	23-Apr-17	5000	6000	8000
A4000	100d	COMMISSIONING & START UP Calendar 7x24hr (24 hours per day)	22-Jul-17	30-Oct-17	1200	2400	3600
A9000	0d	Finish Project		30-Oct-17			

Figure 24 –Translated Min, ML, & Max Duration

To deal with the effect of multiple calendars assigned to Project-A activities, one must use the same settings explained earlier to eliminate the problem of high variances in start/finish dates when compared to the original schedule.

7. Select "Hour" as planning unit in the following OPRA dialog box (Figure 25 - OPRA Import Setting\General Tab Using Hour as the Planning Unit). Check ✅ the square radio button "Use default for new project" if you want the same setting to govern all succeeding imports.

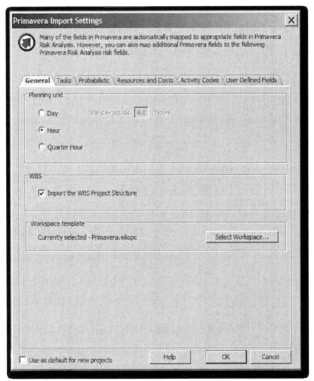

Figure 25 –Import Setting\General

8. We need to define and assign the *Optimistic, Most Likely* and *Pessimistic* durations as user defined custom field data in P6, to map into OPRA during import. Select the already defined duration ranges custom fields in the following import mapping dialog box in OPRA. Check the button that says- "Primavera Values have been entered in hours" (**Figure 26** - OPRA Import Setting\Tasks Tab-Using Hour as the unit of Entry). Check ✅ "Use default for new project" if you want the same setting to govern for all succeeding XER imports.

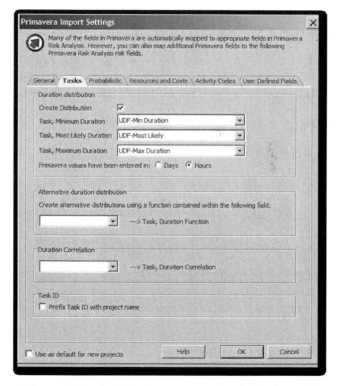

Figure 26 – OPRA Import Setting\Tasks Tab

9. Upon pressing OK, the import process will commence. It will generate a log after import is completed. The OPRA User can choose a specific project directory where to save it (**Figure 27** - OPRA Import Warning Report Log). It is important to check this log file first after every import, even before the Import Check tab as it shows right off the bat any information that was changed. Address any activity attribute that has drastically changed. The log indicated that OPRA has not made any change to Project A. You may continue!

Figure 27 – OPRA Import Warning Report Log

10. On the Menu, click on "Plan\Plan Option." Most medium size and above project schedules will run for several months to years. The project need to see time measures in hours and minutes. On the other hand, a turn around and maintenance schedule that runs for three weeks and less will have set the duration unit by hours. For considerable size projects, use and follow Figure 28 - Check/Correct date setting.

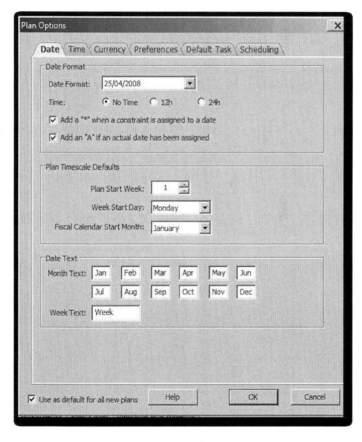

Figure 28 – Check/Correct date setting

137

11. Upon completion of import to OPRA, save as a Risk plan file in your project directory.

Click the "Import Check" tab in OPRA and check for considerable variances in Activity's Start and Finish Dates compared to the Original P6 schedule dates. Ideal is zero variance on all activities.

Some +1 day and -1 day variances are generally tolerable. The analyst must make the call whether it is or not, whether the import quality is acceptable.

The first OPRA schedule dates to check are the key contract deliverables. They should be the same as the original schedule, which means the original deterministic dates of the activities and the corresponding

OPRA dates of the same activities are the same. The import check variance columns must be empty indicating zero variance!

Figure 29 - Project-A Import Check shows that OPRA's Start and Finish Dates are aligned.

The import translation of Project-A schedule data was successful. It shows perfect alignment to the deterministic dates of the original schedule coming from Primavera.

All the take-off points match the deterministic data.

It is time to start the schedule risk quantification process by running OPRA. Since the data quality is excellent, the results are expected to be reliable. The schedule model is therefore a realistic representation of schedule uncertainty, of schedule risk.

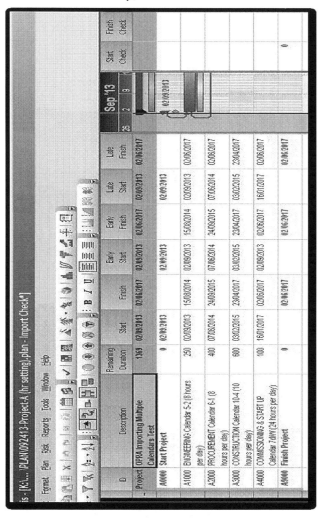

Figure 29 –Import Check

Set the number of iteration. Pick a good number. To see a quick result, you can assign any number from 200 to 500. If you want to fine-tune, choose any number from 500 to 2000. Set quantification above 2000 to as high as 5000+ iterations when doing the final run (**Figure 30**).

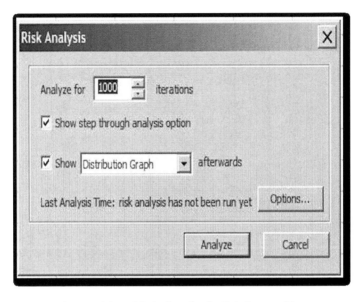

Figure 30 – Risk Analysis Dialogue Box

12. Click on Options button and choose the Risk Data tab. Since Cost component is not part of this quantification, put a check mark on Calculate Duration Sensitivity.

    Calculate Risk Percentiles and Save Resource Data (Figure 31 - OPRA Risk Analysis Options-Risk Data Tab Dialogue Box).

Figure 31 – Risk Analysis Options\Risk Data

13. Choose the Analysis tab and put a check on the radio button shown below including the activation of the Distribution Graph (**Figure 32** - OPRA Risk Options\Analysis Tab Dialogue Box).

Figure 32 – Risk Options\Analysis

14. Click on the Warnings tab. Inspect and make sure that all buttons have a check mark (**Figure 33 -** OPRA Risk Analysis Options-Warnings Tab Dialogue Box).

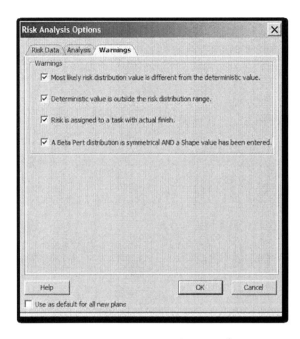

Figure 33 – Risk Analysis Options\Warnings

15. Start iteration by clicking OK. The tool will simulate the schedule risk model.

There might be some warning at the end, like the following examples. Read the message and try to address the warning if needed. Some of the warnings might not be critical and be accepted by clicking OK.

The User must make that call, deciding as to what is most reasonable. If not acceptable, the issue has to be fixed (**Figure 34**, **Figure 35** and **Figure 36**).

Example 1: Error Message: Check Distribution error

Most Likely value is not the same as the remaining duration

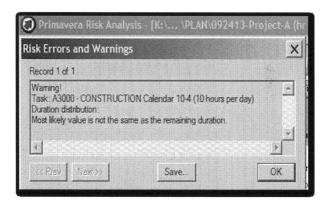

Figure 34 – Risk Errors and Warning 1

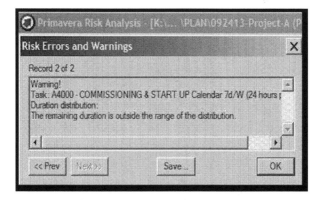

Figure 35 –Risk Errors and Warning 2

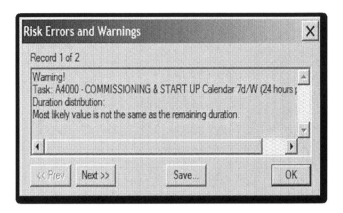

Figure 36 – Risk Errors and Warning 3

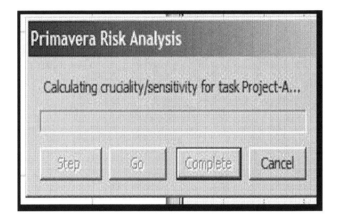

Figure 37 – Calculation Status Box

16. Look at the ranges.

    Make sure that all the three-point estimates for each ranged activity are aligned with the original deterministic schedule (**Figure 38**). Compare value per value manually or do a VLOOKUP using Excel.

144

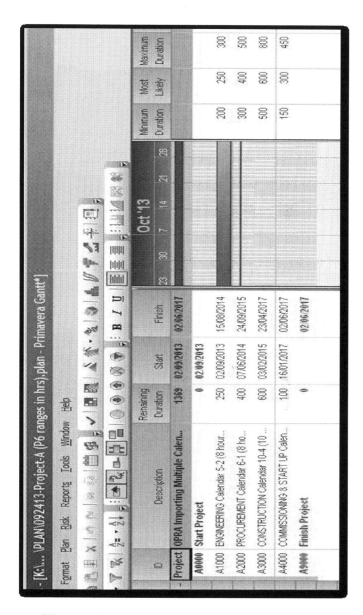

Figure 38 – Review **OPRA** Ranges if correct

17. Change Planning Unit to Days (**Figure 39**)

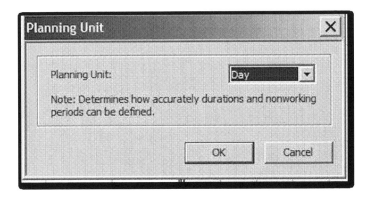

Figure 39 – Planning Unit

18. Distribution Chart 1 (**Figure 40**).

Quick check chart 1!

The Project's Entire Plan deterministic date is aligned to the Original Schedule. It is a good indicator that date translation was good.

19. Distribution Chart 2 (**Figure 41**).

Quick check chart 2!

The Engineering Deterministic Date is aligned to the Original Schedule. It is another good indicator that date translation was good.

20. Distribution Chart 3 (**Figure 42**).

Quick check chart 3! The Construction Deterministic

Date is aligned to the Original Schedule. It is another indicator that date translation is good.

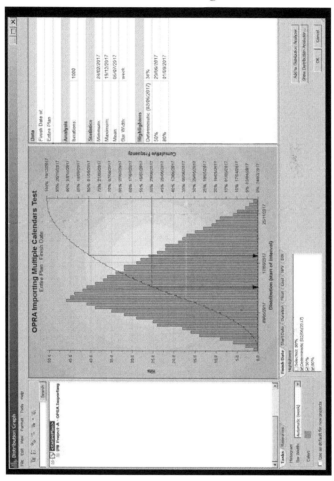

Figure 40 – Distribution Chart 1

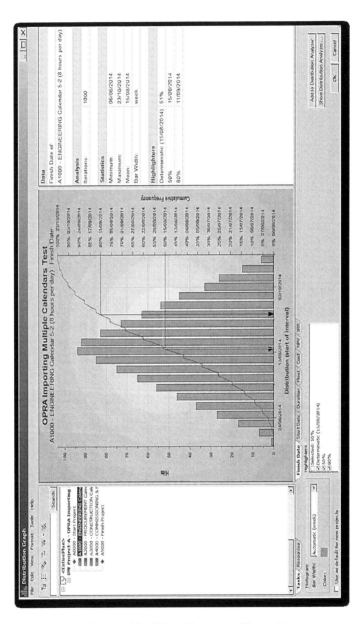

Figure 41 –Distribution Chart 2

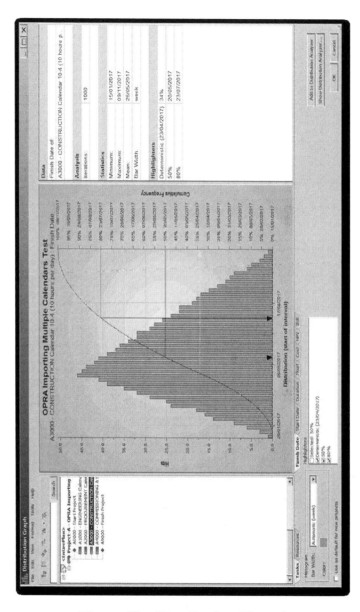

Figure 42 – Distribution Chart 3

21. Distribution Analyzer (**Figure 43**)

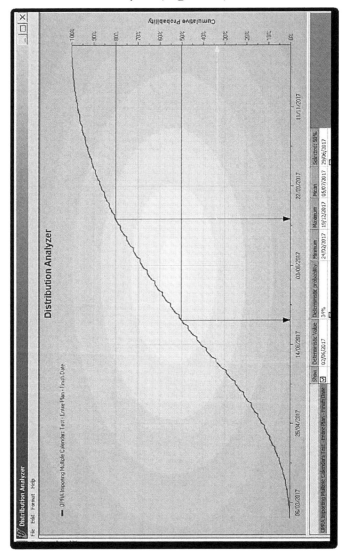

Figure 43 – Distribution Analyzer

22. Make sure that for Multiple Calendars Projects, the "For task durations use Time Periods associated with the task calendar" of the Plan Options\Time Tab is checked (**Figure 44** - Plan Options-Time Tab Dialogue Box).

In this way, the calendar settings govern instead of the Admin default time period.

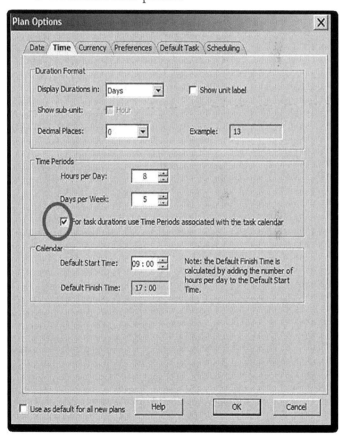

Figure 44 – Plan Options\Time

Always tick the box "For task durations use Time Periods associated with task calendar" to synchronize and align conversion of primavera work hour quantities and durations.

Otherwise, the User will see big variances between the durations and units of original schedule and the OPRA imported schedule.

This is where many would-be analysts fail and will get lost.

Correct setting addresses the following common issues:

- OPRA's activities have bigger durations than P6 original activities but showing the same dates.

- Inputted duration ranges in the Primavera schedule did not translate correctly to OPRA. The values of minimum, most likely and maximum are either bigger, or smaller.

23. Final alignment to be made is in the Plan Option\Scheduling tab.

Ensure that the OPRA setting is the same as the Primavera PPM setting (Figure 46) to remove chances of unreliable results. Note that retained Logic shall be the mandatory setting recommended for all schedules, P6 and OPRA alike (Figure 45).

152

Figure 45 – Schedule Options\Scheduling (OPRA)

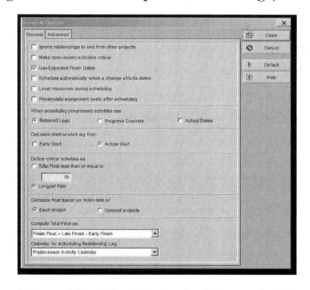

Figure 46 – Schedule Option\General (P6)

38. Copy-Paste

Unknown to many Users, the OPRA tool accommodates the use of copy-paste on all its various activity windows. There are times when the schedule dates in OPRA are all aligned to the original schedule but the duration ranges are in error. Such situations can use the copy-paste solution to capture the right range values.

You can use the copy-paste capability of OPRA to capture the three-point durations from original schedule without converting them to hours. It is easy and simple. You can export the XER from P6 and import the same straight to OPRA. Here are the steps.

1. Open the original schedule using the Primavera tool. Make sure that the duration ranges were already inputted in days to all selected activities.

    Create a filter that will show only the select activities with assigned duration ranges. The risk analyst might say, "let's filter only the activities that were risked."

    It means the same thing. He wanted to display only the activities that have inputs, the duration range or 3-point duration values. The simple P6 filter to use is shown on **Figure 47**. This filter recognizes that the ranges were loaded using users define fields, one of which was called UDF-Max Duration. The filter shall display all remaining activities with the UDF-Max Duration field filled out (active).

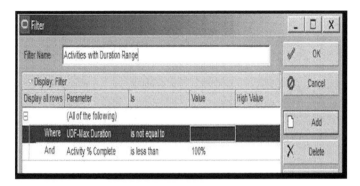

Figure 47 – Filter P6 Activities with duration range

Group activities by WBS or better, do not group at all so it gives a bare list without any grouping. Sort all filtered activities by Activity ID either by ascending or descending order (**Figure 48**). Doing so will show all the risked activities, activities with three-point inputs (**Figure 49 – Filtered and sorted activities**).

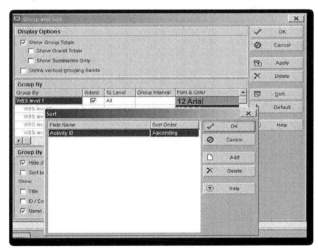

Figure 48 – Group and Sort

Activities

Activity ID	Activity Name	Rem Dur	Start	Finish	Min Duration	Most Likely	Max Duration
032817-Project A		789d	02-Sep-14 A	28-Apr-17			
E1011	Condu:	5d	29-Jun-15	06-Jul-15	3	5d	5
E1022	Condu:	9d	29-Sep-15	13-Oct-15	6	9d	9
E6414	Review	10d	04-May-15	19-May-15	5	10d	10
E6418	Techni:	40d	09-Dec-14 A	12-May-15	18	40d	40
E6419	MR Rei	9d	13-May-15	27-May-15	9	9d	14
E6421	Review	10d	17-Jul-15	31-Jul-15	5	10d	10
ECS1101	Model	36d	13-Apr-15	08-Jun-15	10	36d	36
ECS1106	Model	36d	20-Apr-15	15-Jun-15	10	36d	36
ECS1111	Model	36d	24-Apr-15	19-Jun-15	10	36d	36
ECS3430	Update	18d	02-Dec-15	05-Jan-16	10	18d	20
ECS4260	Model	36d	14-Jul-15	09-Sep-15	30	36d	36
ECS4270	Model	36d	20-Jul-15	15-Sep-15	30	36d	36
ECS4280	Model	36d	27-Jul-15	22-Sep-15	30	36d	36
EIC1190	Develo	99d	02-Jul-15	07-Dec-15	99	99d	171
EIC1270	Update	40d	22-Sep-15	23-Nov-15	20	40d	50
EIC1320	Develo	99d	02-Jul-15	07-Dec-15	99	99d	171
EIC1330	Develo	99d	02-Jul-15	07-Dec-15	60	99d	110
EIC1530	Gener:	27d	24-Nov-15	12-Jan-16	20	27d	40
EIC1750	Prepar	18d	22-Dec-15	26-Jan-16	14	18d	25

Figure 49 – Filtered and sorted activities

2. Click EDIT and Select ALL Activities that were displayed (**Figure 50**).

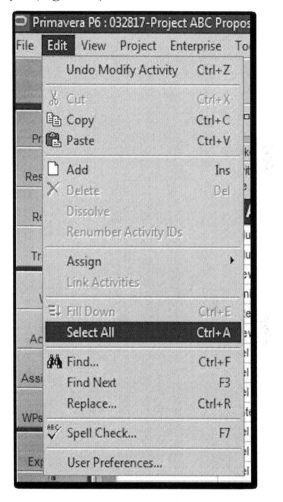

Figure 50 – Select ALL Activities

3. Click COPY after highlighting all filtered activities (**Figure 51**). Get ready to paste it to an Excel file.

Primavera P6 : 032817-Project ABC Proposed BL (032817-Project ABC Proposed BL)

File   Edit   View   Project   Enterprise   Tools   Admin   Help

Edit menu	
Undo Modify Activity	Ctrl+Z
Cut	Ctrl+X
Copy	Ctrl+C
Paste	Ctrl+V
Add	Ins
Delete	Del
Dissolve	
Renumber Activity IDs	
Assign	▶
Link Activities	
Fill Down	Ctrl+E
Select All	Ctrl+A
Find...	Ctrl+F
Find Next	F3
Replace...	Ctrl+R
Spell Check...	F7
User Preferences...	

...ked Activities(Final)   Filter: Any Activities with Dura...

	Rem Dur	Start	Finish	Min Duration	Most Likely	Max Duration
	9d	29-Sep-15	13-Oct-15	6	9d	9
	10d	04-May-15	19-May-15	5	10d	10
	40d	09-Dec-14 A	12-May-15	18	40d	40
	9d	13-May-15	27-May-15	9	9d	14
	10d	17-Jul-15	31-Jul-15	5	10d	10
	36d	13-Apr-15	08-Jun-15	10	36d	36
	36d	20-Apr-15	15-Jun-15	10	36d	36
	36d	24-Apr-15	19-Jun-15	10	36d	36
	18d	02-Dec-15	05-Jan-16	10	18d	20
	36d	14-Jul-15	09-Sep-15	30	36d	36
	36d	20-Jul-15	15-Sep-15	30	36d	36
	36d	27-Jul-15	22-Sep-15	30	36d	38
EIC1320 Develo	99d	02-Jul-15	07-Dec-15	99	99d	171
EIC1330 Develo	99d	02-Jul-15	07-Dec-15	60	99d	110
EIC1530 Generi	27d	24-Nov-15	12-Jan-16	20	27d	40
EIC1750 Prepar	18d	22-Dec-15	26-Jan-16	14	18d	25

Thresholds
Issues

Figure 51 – COPY ALL Activities

4. Open Excel. Go to first available field and PASTE. All copied activities from Primavera will be pasted on the spreadsheet (**Figure 52**). Give it a name and save the file.

Activity ID	Activity Name	Rem Dur	Start	Finish	Min Duration	Most Likely	Max Duration
E1011	Conduct 1st Model Review (Mai	5d	29-Jun-15	6-Jul-15	3	5d	5
E1022	Conduct 2nd Module Model Rev	9d	29-Sep-15	13-Oct-15	6	9d	9
E6414	Review 1st Vendor Data - Bitum	10d	4-May-15	19-May-15	5	10d	10
E6418	Technical Bid Evaluation - Instr.	40d	09-Dec-14 A	12-May-15	18	40d	40
E6419	MR Request for PO - Instr. Air Cc	9d	13-May-15	27-May-15	9	9d	14
E6421	Review 1st Vendor Data - Instr. /	10d	17-Jul-15	31-Jul-15	5	10d	10
ECS1101	Model Process Areas Main Struc	36d	13-Apr-15	8-Jun-15	10	36d	36
ECS1106	Model Process Areas Piling for N	36d	20-Apr-15	15-Jun-15	10	36d	36
ECS1111	Model Process Areas Concrete/I	36d	24-Apr-15	19-Jun-15	10	36d	36
ECS3430	Update & Issue WEG Pump Area	18d	2-Dec-15	5-Jan-16	10	18d	20
ECS4260	Model Process Areas Main Struc	36d	14-Jul-15	9-Sep-15	30	36d	36
ECS4270	Model Process Areas Piling for N	36d	20-Jul-15	15-Sep-15	30	36d	36
ECS4280	Model Process Areas Concrete/I	36d	27-Jul-15	22-Sep-15	30	36d	36
EIC1190	Develop SIS Design	99d	2-Jul-15	7-Dec-15	99	99d	171
EIC1270	Update Control Narratives (For t	40d	22-Sep-15	23-Nov-15	20	40d	50
EIC1320	Develop DCS Design & Configur	99d	2-Jul-15	7-Dec-15	99	99d	171
EIC1330	Develop Control & Communicat	99d	2-Jul-15	7-Dec-15	60	99d	110
EIC1530	Generate & Issue Network Dwgs	27d	24-Nov-15	12-Jan-16	20	27d	40
EIC1750	Prepare & Issue Control System:	18d	22-Dec-15	26-Jan-16	14	18d	25

Figure 52 – PASTE ALL Activities to Excel

5. Export XER of the original schedule to an accessible directory. Import that same XER to OPRA. Open the schedule in OPRA (Figure 53) displaying Minimum, Most Likely, and Maximum duration columns. Filter, group, sort the activities using the same filter, group, and sort settings that was used in P6 (Figure 54). This is done to prepare OPRA activity window for pasting the three-point values straight from the Excel file. The display should be the same in P6 activity window, in Excel, and in OPRA. Do not just paste the values unless this check was done.

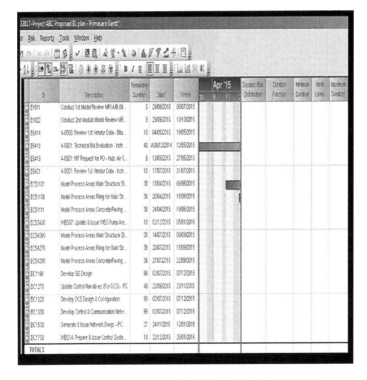

Figure 53 – Open the Schedule in OPRA

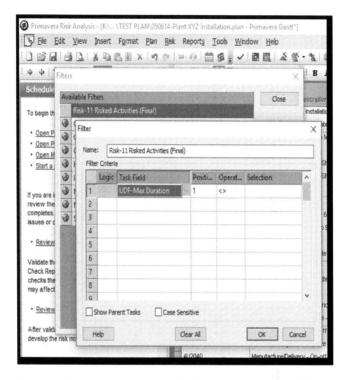

Figure 54 – Same Group & Sort Setting in OPRA

6. While the schedule is open in OPRA, go back to your Excel file.

7. Select the Minimum, Most Likely and Maximum fields of all listed activities (**Figure 55**).

8. Press COPY. You have just copied all the three-point durations to your temporary clip-board, ready for pasting.

	A	B	C	D	E	F	G	H
1	Activity ID	Activity Name	Rem Dur	Start	Finish	Min Duration	Most Likely	Max Duration
2	E1011	Conduct 1st Model Review (Mai	5d	29-Jun-15	6-Jul-15	3	5d	5
3	E1022	Conduct 2nd Module Model Rev	9d	29-Sep-15	13-Oct-15	6	9d	9
4	E6414	Review 1st Vendor Data - Bitum	10d	4-May-15	19-May-15	5	10d	10
5	E6418	Technical Bid Evaluation - Instr.	40d	09-Dec-14 A	12-May-15	18	40d	40
6	E6419	MR Request for PO - Instr. Air Cc	9d	13-May-15	27-May-15	9	9d	14
7	E6421	Review 1st Vendor Data - Instr. /	10d	17-Jul-15	31-Jul-15	5	10d	10
8	ECS1101	Model Process Areas Main Struc	36d	13-Apr-15	8-Jun-15	10	36d	36
9	ECS1106	Model Process Areas Piling for N	36d	20-Apr-15	15-Jun-15	10	36d	36
10	ECS1111	Model Process Areas Concrete/I	36d	24-Apr-15	19-Jun-15	10	36d	36
11	ECS3430	Update & Issue WEG Pump Area	18d	2-Dec-15	5-Jan-16	10	18d	20
12	ECS4260	Model Process Areas Main Struc	36d	14-Jul-15	9-Sep-15	30	36d	36
13	ECS4270	Model Process Areas Piling for N	36d	20-Jul-15	15-Sep-15	30	36d	36
14	ECS4280	Model Process Areas Concrete/I	36d	27-Jul-15	22-Sep-15	30	36d	36
15	EIC1190	Develop SIS Design	99d	2-Jul-15	7-Dec-15	99	99d	171
16	EIC1270	Update Control Narratives (For L	40d	22-Sep-15	23-Nov-15	20	40d	50
17	EIC1320	Develop DCS Design & Configura	99d	2-Jul-15	7-Dec-15	99	99d	171
18	EIC1330	Develop Control & Communicat	99d	2-Jul-15	7-Dec-15	60	99d	110
19	EIC1530	Generate & Issue Network Dwg:	27d	24-Nov-15	12-Jan-16	20	27d	40
20	EIC1750	Prepare & Issue Control System:	18d	22-Dec-15	26-Jan-16	14	18d	25

Figure 55 – Select and Copy the ranges from Excel

9. Go back to OPRA activity window; whichever tab you prefer. I suggest that you stick to the first tab called Primavera Gantt. Select the first field at the top under the header Minimum Duration and PASTE what was copied from Excel (**Figure 56**). The values will automatically populate all the fields in the right order (**Figure 57**).

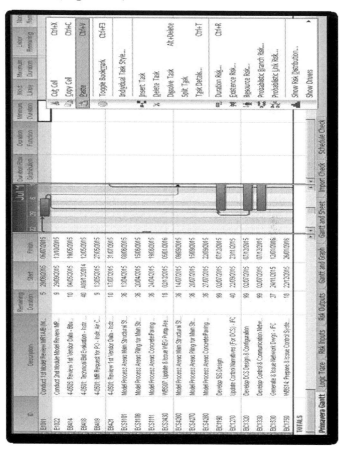

Figure 56 – Select the first field and paste

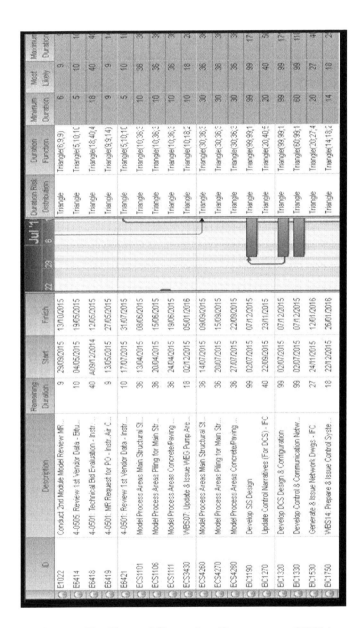

Figure 57 – Pasted Duration Ranges on OPRA

164

10. If you want to change the Duration Risk Distribution (Duration Function) to another instead of the Triangle (default), change the first occurrence and do a fill down. In **Figure 58**, the analyst wanted to change Triangle distribution to Trigen. **Figure 59** shows that he has successfully made the change.

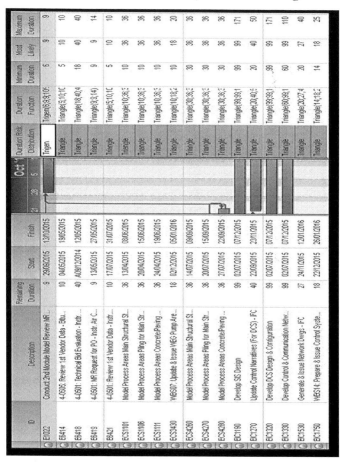

Figure 58 – Triangle changed to Trigen

165

ID	Description	Remaining Duration	Start	Finish			Duration Risk Distribution
E1011	Conduct 1st Model Review MR1 A...	3	25/06/2015	30/06/2015			Trigen
E1022	Conduct 2nd Module Model Revie...	6	07/10/2015	15/10/2015			Trigen
E6414	4-0505: Review 1st Vendor Data ...	7	28/04/2015	07/05/2015			Trigen
E6418	4-0501: Technical Bid Evaluation ...	21	A 09/12/2014	21/05/2015			Trigen
E6419	4-0501: MR Request for PO - Inst...	12	22/05/2015	09/06/2015			Trigen
E6421	4-0501: Review 1st Vendor Data ...	2	22/07/2015	23/07/2015			Trigen
ECS1101	Model Process Areas Main Struct...	32	16/04/2015	05/06/2015			Trigen
ECS1106	Model Process Areas Piling for M...	36	16/04/2015	11/06/2015			Trigen
ECS1111	Model Process Areas Concrete/P...	36	23/04/2015	18/06/2015			Trigen
ECS3430	WBS07: Update & Issue WEG Pu...	17	14/12/2015	14/01/2016			Trigen
ECS4260	Model Process Areas Main Struct...	33	27/07/2015	16/09/2015			Trigen
ECS4270	Model Process Areas Piling for M...	22	19/08/2015	23/09/2015			Trigen
ECS4280	Model Process Areas Concrete/P...	47	16/07/2015	29/09/2015			Trigen
EIC1190	Develop SIS Design	107	18/06/2015	07/12/2015			Trigen
EIC1270	Update Control Narratives (For D...	31	29/09/2015	17/11/2015			Trigen
EIC1320	Develop DCS Design & Configura...	132	18/06/2015	21/01/2016			Trigen
EIC1330	Develop Control & Communication...	94	19/08/2015	21/01/2016			Trigen
EIC1530	Generate & Issue Network Dwgs...	27	11/01/2016	19/02/2016			Trigen
EIC1750	WBS14: Prepare & Issue Control ...	23	29/01/2016	04/03/2016			Trigen

Figure 59 – Copy-Fill Trigen Distribution

39. SQRA Report

39.1 SQRA Report Format

Schedule risk analysis does not necessarily have to be very long and extremely detailed. The report is created to present the findings to stakeholders, most particularly to the decision makers.

It is a good method of demonstrating quantified risks, whether it be a threat or an opportunity to the company. The report must be clear, succinct, and complete.

I've come across a voluminous reports generated and expanded by an exceedingly expensive third-party consultant but clients don't read them for the most part.

In the end, the receiver would only read the summary report of probability and schedule contingency, disregarding whatever got them there. Customers tend to demand the bottom line assessment and ignore the details.

While the detailed report holds many important aspects of the findings, including the recommended solutions, they seldom get the attention they need.

In effect, the recommendations don't get carried out nor addressed seriously. It is a challenge that makes detail-oriented risk analysts feel extremely nervous and ineffective.

The company is best advised to tap into the services of their in-house central team comprised of risk subject matter experts. Given the right people on the job, the result will be more insightful.

Between a 300-page report and a 30-page report, the latter might be the better deal because it can be digested in one reading. Much of the 300-page report stays unread. The report can be in Word or PPT format. The succeeding sections show an SQRA result using the power point format.

39.2   Front – Cover Page

The cover page of an SQRA report should include the name of the project, what stage it is in, a company logo, the name of the risk analyst who prepared the report, the date when the report was prepared, and the revision number.

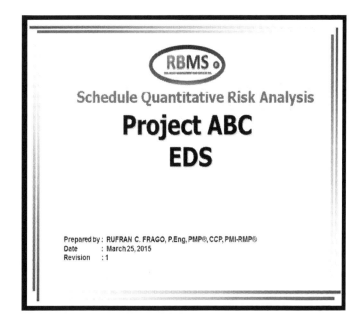

Figure 60 – Cover Page

39.3   Slide 1 – Purpose

The specific purpose of this specific SQRA must be enumerated on this page. Only items the project wishes to focus on should be included.

It is comprises schedule contingency and probability figures of some select activities and milestones or just the project's last deliverable such as First Oil or Ready for Operation.

Typically included are the identifications of schedule drivers, criticality charts, and sensitivity tornado charts.

Slide 1: Purpose

1. To determine the overall schedule contingency of Project ABC based on April 28, 2017 FIRST OIL.
2. To calculate the probability of completing Project ABC Project FIRST OIL on April 28, 2017.
3. To calculate the probability of achieving Project ABC Project select KPI Milestones' deterministic dates.
4. To identify schedule drivers sitting on the dynamic critical path and the associated risks requiring treatments.
5. To calculate schedule sensitivities through the resulting criticality charts and graphs.
6. To use outputs as inputs in finalizing Project ABC Official Schedule Baseline.

Figure 61 – Slide 1 Purpose Page

39.4   Slide 2 – Key Milestones

The analyst must sit down with the project manager and ask for their most important key performance milestones and activities. These milestones are usually taken into consideration along with the contracts in play.

Automatically included on the list is the final deliverable.

The points of concern will vary among stakeholders depending on the type of role and responsibility they have. Individual interest is different.

If the project manager is responsible only for the EPC budget, he might want to exclude commissioning and start-up from the picture. If this becomes the case, his last milestone will be the final turnover.

The risk analyst, however, has the professional duty of suggesting that an integrated approach is the best practice to follow whenever possible.

Slide 2: Key Performance Milestones

ACTIVITY ID	KEY PERFORMANCE MILESTONES	DETERMINISTIC DATE
KM1250	Award PO Pipe Fabrication	17-Mar-15
KM1220	1st Model Review - Tank Lot and Piperack	21-May-15
KM1240	Award PO Structural Steel	08-Jun-15
KM1280	2nd Model Review - Tank Lot and Piperack	11-Aug-15
KM1230	Issue P&ID IFC	20-Aug-15
KM1210	1st Model Review - Process Area	24-Aug-15
KM1270	2nd Model Review - Process Area	30-Nov-15
KM1020	Install Piling - NE Tank Farm	05-Dec-15
KM1260	Award PO Substation / EHouse 2&3	17-Dec-15
KM1030	Install Foundations - NE Tank Farm	18-Jan-16
KM1290	3rd Model Review - Process Area	05-Feb-16
KM1310	Delivery (Hot Facility) Drain Tank	01-Mar-16
KM1300	Delivery of VCU Package	06-Apr-16
KM1040	Install Piling - Blended Bitumen Area	16-Jun-16
KM1050	Install Foundations - Blended Bitumen Area	26-Jul-16
KM1100	TCCC LP Natural Gas	30-Aug-16
KM1320	Delivery Substation	06-Oct-16
KM1120	TCCC Vent Gas	01-Nov-16
KM1060	TCCC Electrical 35kV	05-Jan-17
KM1070	TCCC Electrical 4160V	05-Jan-17
KM1080	TCCC Electrical 480V	05-Jan-17
KM1110	TCCC Instrument Air	24-Jan-17
KM1130	First Oil (FO)	28-Apr-17

Figure 62 – Slide 2 Key Performance Milestones

39.5   Slide 3 – Primary Data

Primary data refers to given data. It talks about the model's working information or source data. It describes how the sample was sliced and diced, and how the sampling population was represented. This section is relevant because it gives the readers sufficient background knowledge about the inputs used in the simulation.

Information such as when SQRA was conducted, the name of the project schedule, its data date, and tool version can be valuable later on when certain issues come up relevant thereto. The statistical breakdown of activities according to attributes provides the audience and the analyst a summed up feel and preview of the landscape.

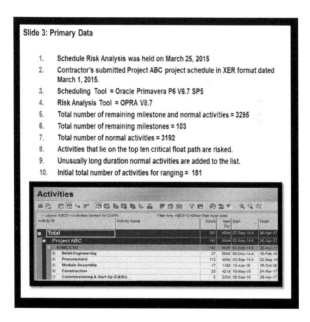

Figure 63 – Slide 3 Primary Data

39.6   Slide 4 – Schedule Quality Check

A major prerequisite to running schedule risk analysis is making sure that the quality of the schedule meets the company's governing minimum criteria. A good quality schedule is a critical prerequisite of any successful quantitative exercise.

The filter, group, and sort features of Primavera Project Management or any scheduling tool can be used to come up with the schedule quality metrics and a corresponding score.

Each score will then have to be compared to the minimum benchmark score. If the score or combination score passes the benchmark or total benchmark score respectively, the schedule is deemed fit for SQRA.

Slide 4: Schedule Quality Check

1. The schedule has generally good activity durations, sequence, project structures, and groupings aligned to the current plan and strategy.
2. Construction schedule follows the path of construction.
3. C&SU drives construction.
4. Construction drives all upstream activities.
5. All essential and influential project stakeholders/representative of the project management team have reviewed and agreed to the proposed deterministic schedule and relevant key milestone dates.
6. This is an integrated schedule that includes scope of other contractors.
7. The schedule contains key interphases.
8. The schedule met Client's Schedule Ready for Risk requirement.
9. Deltek Acumen Fuse schedule quality analyzer tool is used. The summary quality ribbons are shown in Slide 15.
10. The overall quality score passed the activity-based score set by the client. Client minimum quality requires a score above 70%.
11. Schedule risks already quantified in the risk register will not be used as reckoning information in this quantification to avoid double-dipping.

Figure 64 – Slide 4 Schedule Quality Check

39.7   Slide 5 – Activities Selection Criteria

Traditional method of schedule risk analysis calls for the identification of activities to be ranged. These activities follow the selection criteria that makes the most sense. The report has to explain the method of selection so that the project understands the launching foundation of the simulation.

Risk analysts must strive to come up with a good representative list of the most plausible activities representing all critical, near critical, and potentially critical activities.

The following criteria are a great example.

1.   Filter all remaining normal activities included in the top ten critical float paths.

2.   Add to the list all activities with remaining duration greater than 90 days. Reason: Overall project duration is more sensitive to longer duration activities.

3.   Adding the result of 1 and 2 generates a list of 175 activities.

4.   This list of activities is extracted from static multiple critical paths.

Allow project members who participated in the risk analysis session to suggest other normal activities they believe should be part of the critical list.

The SMEs identified six activities. Total number of activities to be ranged = 181

5. Activity duration ranges are based on personal and group interviews using the Delphi Interview Sheet and the facilitated approach.

6. Interview sheets (**Figure 15**) are sent to responsible EPMC/C&SU disciplines and managers provide additional time to the participants to make sure that inputs are accurate. This helps the risk analyst to prepare a better SRA model.

7. This risk model using Latin Hypercube simulation applied to a Trigen distribution profile of P10/P90 is preferred by many.

Slide 5: Selecting the activities to be ranged

1. Filter all remaining normal activities included in the top ten critical float paths.
2. Add to the list all activities with remaining duration greater than 90 days. Reason: Overall project duration is more sensitive to longer duration activities.
3. Adding the result of 1 and 2 generates a list of 175 activities.
4. Since the list of activities is extracted from static multiple critical paths, project members who participated in the risk analysis session are allowed to suggest other normal activities they believe should be part of the critical list to be risked based on their experience. The SMEs identified six activities. Total number of activities to be ranged = 181
5. Activity duration ranges are based on personal and group interviews using Delphi Interview Sheet and the facilitated approach.
6. Interview sheets sent to responsible EPMC/C&SU disciplines and managers provides additional time to the participants to make a more accurate inputs. It helps the risk analyst to prepare a better SRA model.
7. This risk model uses Latin Hypercube simulation applied to TRIGEN distribution profile of P10/P90 as prescribed by the new ADEM procedure of quantification to derive results.

Slide 6: Report Document Distribution
Note that this report has confidential information and distribution is limited.

Figure 65 – Slide 5 Filtering Criteria

174

39.8   Slide 6 – Precaution on Report Distribution

There is a precaution regarding report distribution because it is a controlled process. Distribute the results of risk analysis only to select stakeholders in order to be more effective and retain confidentiality. These project members have the knowledge, authority, and responsibility to decide, act, and provide direction.

Indiscriminately publishing the results can result in a breach of confidentiality. They could leak to an outside party and affect the company's standing and competitive advantage.

```
Slide 6: Report Document Distribution
   Note that this report has confidential information and distribution is limited.
```

Figure 66 – Slide 6 Filtering Criteria

It would be wise for the analyst to ask his leader who should receive the SQRA report. Never send the report out to all project members. Be cautiously selective!

39.9   Slide 7 – Input Template

Subject matter experts shall fill out a form to give their three-point range inputs for each activity within their expertise. The form should be an Excel file developed by the analyst and distributed to the project leads.

In our Project ABC example, the analyst has identified 181 activities to range. The input sheets containing the activities were received back from the responsible disciplines. They were consolidated by the lead planners and schedulers and forwarded to the risk analyst, who then uploaded the information to the risk analysis tool; e.g. OPRA.

Slide 7 of the report does not intend to collect full detailed information. It only shows what a typical table template looks like and what suggested data points it must contain. The column headers should include the following (starting from the leftmost column). Note that the field's list below was generated from Primavera. They can be pasted straight into Excel from Primavera P6, automatically distributing the data on respective rows and columns.

1. Activity ID
2. Activity Name (Activity Description)
3. Activity Count
4. Remaining Duration
5. Start Date
6. Finish Date
7. Budgeted Labor Units
8. Remaining Labor Units
9. At Completion Labor Units
10. Minimum Duration
11. Most Likely Duration
12. Maximum Duration
13. Resources
14. Budgeted Non-Labor Units
15. At Completion Non-Labor Units

16. Risk Filter

17. Short Description of Considered Risk

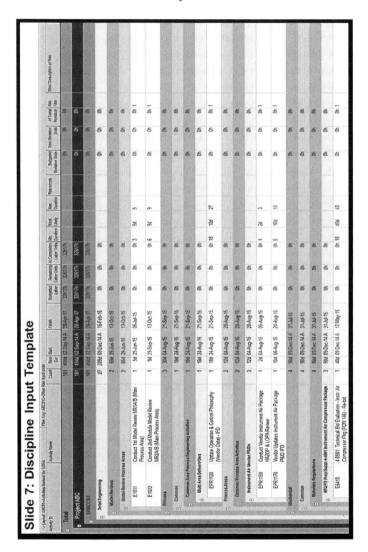

Figure 67 – Input Worksheet

177

39.10   Slide 8 – Participants

The list of participants who provided input is a vital background information that gives the report more credibility.

The report's message and recommendation are deemed more reliable by management when they know that the inputs came from a representative cross-section of subject matter experts.

One-on-one interviews with the SMEs can add to their objectivity. The opportunity of giving expert judgment without being influenced by bosses gives more credence to the input. It reinforces the notion that the inputs are actually theirs. It makes the SQRA output more acceptable.

As long as the disciplines understand the three-point range philosophy and the correct working perspective, a final review of the ranges comes easy. If not, it becomes a struggle.

An example of this is when SMEs try to dissect activities into such minute details that it defeats what could have been a worthwhile exercise.

Warning indicators that might jeopardize the traditional process of three-point duration ranging are:

1. SMEs cannot decide if there is enough certainty to daylong duration activities.

    This usually happens when an SME intends to build contingency on each activity instead of using objective assessment of the task.

If digging three holes on the ground takes less than a day, why would anyone say it is a 1, 2, 3 range?

Such an activity under a normal, no-risk situation is quite certain.

From a pure, estimating point of view, a three-point range applied to such activities does not make good sense.

2. Short duration activities lying on the same activity chain are all ranged.

Blanket ranging is not a good idea. Selective ranging is the right way.

3. The sample schedule is already outdated (stale schedule).

SQRA is most relevant and useful when the schedule under analysis has not passed one update cycle.

The closer it is to the last data date, the better it is.

4. Managers and directors provide the ranges instead of the frontline disciplines.

The tendency to baby the project might result.

This can bring management biases to the forefront.

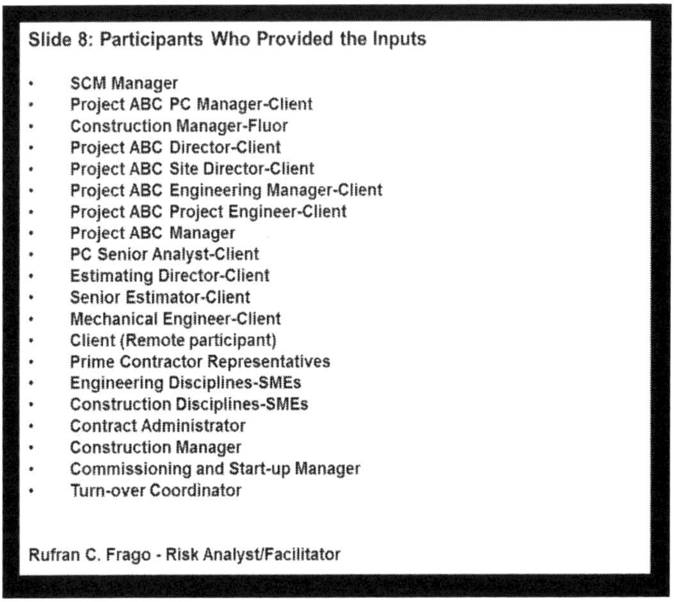

Figure 68 – Slide 8 Participants

39.11 Slide 9 – Static Critical Path

This slide provides a photo-grab of the primary critical path of the schedule being analyzed before the start of the SQRA. It is used to contrast the quantified criticality result and the static path produced from the deterministic schedule. Through this, the recipients of the report will grasp in full the importance of identifying the dynamic critical path.

Critical paths are more dynamic in nature than static. It constantly changes with each schedule update even activities with high criticality can switch path. Some might even end up as non-critical.

What we can filter from our P6 schedule are static critical paths. They are essentially just a snapshot of the path in time. That snapshot is equivalent to a singular iteration run, using our risk analysis tool. Never rely on this indicator with blind confidence. Always crosscheck with periodic schedule risk analysis.

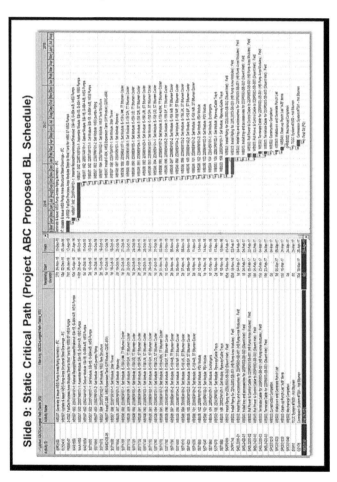

Figure 69 – Slide 9 Static Critical Path

39.12   Slide 10 – Previous Sensitivity Analysis

Sensitivity analysis conducted in the more recent past can be a source of good information. It can also be a benchmark of some sort needed to appreciate schedule changes and updates. It does not matter whether the analysis was done by the contractor or the client.

The risk analyst must be able to screen out useful data that might add some dimension to an upcoming SQRA. If no previous analysis is available, it is recommended to mention it in your slides.

Figure 70 – Slide 10 Past Sensitivity Analysis

39.13   Slide 11 – Top 10 Schedule Drivers

This section shall list the top schedule drivers as derived from the resulting tornado charts.

The analyst has to understand what each tornado group signifies.

The following guide can facilitate the identification of the top ten activities:

> Choose activities common to more than one tornado group.

The greater the number of times an activity is repeated, the more critical managing the activity will be in the project schedule.

> Focus more on upstream activities.

Downstream activities more often than not show up as critical because they are downstream at the bottleneck of everything upstream.

> Project teams have more information and definition during upstream works, so addressing them leads to more effective management.

Improving the activities to the left improves the probability of deliverables to the right.

ACTIVITY ID	DESCRIPTION	LEGEND
• MAA1650	Assemble Module: E&I-1B, G-884 A/B, Pumps	3
• P5838	Fab/Deliver to Mod Yard - UPS & DC System	2
• MA01650	Material Receipt/Warehouse/Shakeout: E&I-1B, G-884 A/B, Pumps	1
• P5210	Eng/Fab/Assembly/Install/Wiring/Test – Substation	2
• O2176	Commission System #7591	1
• P6888-07	Fab/Del Process Area Modules Steel to Mod Yard for WBS 07	1
• P5571	Evaluate and Award PO – Instrument Air Compressor Pkg	1
• SKPP1740	Install Piping for 220L0003-SB-001 (HB Pump Area Modules)	1
• P3420	Vendor Prepare 1st Vendor Data – Inst Air Compressor Pkg	1
• SKPP2490	Install Piping for 220L0003-SB-002 (Diluent Inlet)	1

LEGEND:
1= included in the top ten critical path
2= belongs to the long duration activities of greater than or equal to 20 days
3= not included in category 1 and 2

Figure 71 – Slide 11 Schedule Drivers

39.14   Slide 12 – Schedule Risk Analysis Summary

This SQRA summary points to the most important project milestone or activity. For a construction outfit and the client, this is typically the last construction activity. It is the turnover activity.

For other oil and gas construction projects, the focus might be on First Oil, as it represents the first standard commercial barrel of oil produced. Whatever the case may be, this particular slide should capture what the project manager and his leaders need to see.

The example below identifies First Oil (FO) as the most important milestone.

A short probability distribution report was provided.

It shows that the date difference measured from the deterministic finish date and the company's standard risk appetite of P70 corresponds to the measure of schedule contingency.

There are twenty-four (24) weeks of schedule contingency to achieve 70% probability.

 The above risked dates are not the "worst case" but a normal case scenario. The date ranges used in the analysis did not address catastrophic events.

In short, there is no confidence that Project ABC's First Oil will be successfully delivered on time.

The target date of April 28, 2017 is not achievable.

The schedule has to be reviewed, fast-tracked some more, or perhaps optimized to improve probability.

FIRST OIL (FO)

Maximum duration:	12Jan2018	Chance: P100%
Risk simulated Finish:	14Oct2017	Chance: P70%
Deterministic duration:	28Apr2017	Chance: <P1%

Note : Risk date differences must be measured from the Deterministic Finish date. The delta between Client Standard P70 and Deterministic date is called Schedule Risk Contingency; i.e. 24-weeks.

The above risked dates are not "worst case" but a normal case scenario. The date ranges used in the analysis did not address catastrophic events.

Interpretation

FIRST OIL for this project has a 70% chance of finishing 24-weeks from the deterministic finish date of 28Apr17. In brief, there is no confidence that the Project ABC First Oil will be successfully delivered on time. Target date is not achievable. The schedule has to be reviewed, fast-tracked some more or optimized to improve probability. See detailed recommendation.

Figure 72 – Slide 12 SQRA Summary

39.15   Slide 13 – Key Milestones/Activities

Other key milestones and activities are also important to look at. They are essential points in the schedule that can add value to the monitoring and control process.

Slide 13: SQRA SUMMARY ON KEY MILESTONES/ACTIVITIES

ACTIVITY ID	KEY MILESTONES	DETERMINISTIC DATE	DETERMINISTIC PROBABILITY	P50 DATE	P70 DATE
KMS1250	Award PO Pipe Fabrication	17-Mar-15	100%	17-Mar-15	17-Mar-15
KMS1220	1st Model Review - Tank Lot and Piperack	21-May-15	100%	21-May-15	21-May-15
KMS1240	Award PO Structural Steel	08-Jun-15	100%	08-Jun-15	08-Jun-15
KMS1280	2nd Model Review - Tank Lot and Piperack	11-Aug-15	100%	11-Aug-15	11-Aug-15
KMS1230	Issue P&ID IFC	20-Aug-15	22%	02-Sep-15	14-Sep-15
KMS1210	1st Model Review - Process Area	24-Aug-15	99%	24-Aug-15	24-Aug-15
KMS1270	2nd Model Review - Process Area	30-Nov-15	63%	30-Nov-15	02-Dec-15
KMS1020	Install Piling - NE Tank Farm	05-Dec-15	100%	05-Dec-15	05-Dec-15
KMS1260	Award PO Substation / EHouse 2&3	17-Dec-15	95%	17-Dec-15	17-Dec-15
KMS1030	Install Foundations - NE Tank Farm	18-Jan-16	100%	18-Jan-16	18-Jan-16
KMS1290	3rd Model Review - Process Area	05-Feb-16	63%	05-Feb-16	09-Feb-16
KMS1310	Delivery (Hot Facility) Drain Tank	01-Mar-16	12%	30-Mar-16	15-Apr-16
KMS1300	Delivery of VCU Package	06-Apr-16	2%	30-May-16	14-Jun-16
KMS1040	Install Piling - Blended Bitumen Area	16-Jun-16	80%	16-Jun-16	16-Jun-16
KMS1050	Install Foundations - Blended Bitumen Area	26-Jul-16	80%	26-Jul-16	26-Jul-16
KMS1100	TCCC LP Natural Gas	30-Aug-16	Less than 1%	07-Nov-16	23-Nov-16
KMS1320	Delivery Substation	06-Oct-16	7%	16-Dec-16	18-Jan-17
KMS1120	TCCC Vent Gas	01-Nov-16	12%	29-Nov-16	18-Dec-16
KMS1060	TCCC Electrical 35kV	05-Jan-17	18%	02-Mar-17	06-Apr-17
KMS1070	TCCC Electrical 4160V	05-Jan-17	18%	02-Mar-17	06-04-17
KMS1080	TCCC Electrical 480V	05-Jan-17	18%	02-Mar-17	06-Apr-17
KMS1110	TCCC Instrument Air	24-Jan-17	Less than 1%	29-May-17	19-Jun-17
KMS1130	First Oil (FO)	28-Apr-17	Less than 1%	19-Sep-17	14-Oct-17

Figure 73 – Slide 13 Key Milestones/Activities

39.16   Slide 14 – Schedule Quality Assessment

A control schedule should pass quality assessment based on approved quality benchmarks.

This is necessary to make sure that schedule analysis will come up with meaningful results.

By attaining or exceeding the set schedule quality, the project can mitigate inherent schedule risks.

Since the schedule serves as the primary input data to SQRA, it is common sense to place schedule quality in high regard. The higher its quality, the more reliable the quantified risk result will be and vice-versa.

There are schedule quality analysis tools available to help evaluate the schedule's readiness.

Once a scoring rule and metric benchmarks are established, the tool of choice will do most of the heavy lifting.

Figure **74** shows a Deltek Acumen Fuse summary dashboard. The specific metrics are totaled to give an overall score.

In this case, the overall score based on activity metrics equals 74%.

The passing score in this case requires that minimum quality be above 70% (see Section 39.6).

The project can come up with their own passing benchmark.

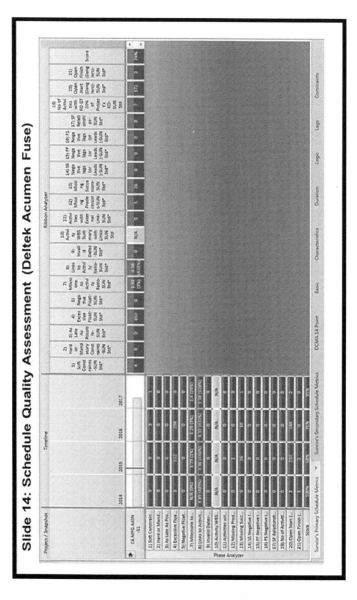

Figure 74 – Slide 14 Quality Assessment Summary

189

39.17   Slide 15 – Schedule Check

An OPRA schedule check summary is a high-level supporting page on schedule quality. It is an important page for the analyst, who does not have the Deltek Acumen Fuse quality analysis tool. For those who have Acumen Fuse or similar tool, this slide might not be necessary except to crosscheck results.

A good tool can be configured to check constraints, out of sequence activities, leads and lags, SF links, links to summary tasks, open-ended activities, out of sequence progress, danglers, and many others. The schedule check report checks a schedule for common problems that may affect a deterministic plan and/or a risk analysis.

The justification for each check is viewable and editable in the "Rationale" tab of the Schedule Check Options dialog box. Once changes to the rationale text, click "Apply" to save (Primavera Risk Analysis Help, 2000).

You can choose to select a different rationale using the drop down menu. Reset in the Rationale tab will reset the text for the selected Rationale. "Reset All Rationale" will reset all text in every saved rationale.

Once more, let me take this opportunity to underline the tremendous effects of schedule constraints to the risk analysis results when used excessively or not according to project plan and strategy.

They should be used in accordance with the risk model at play and though easier said than done, must reflect one that is realistic. It should be a serious consideration for the project to remove constraints by replacing them with logic ties instead.

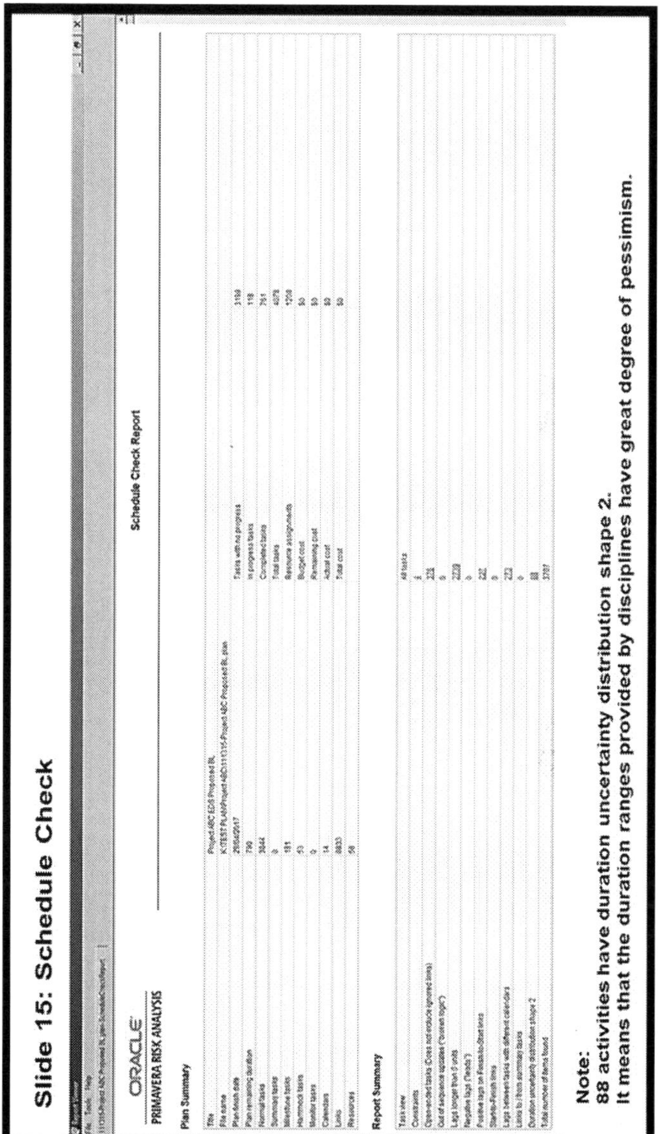

Figure 75 – Slide 15 Schedule Check by OPRA

39.18 Slide 16 – Disclaimer

A disclaimer page is generally a statement intended to specify or delimit the responsibility of the analyst. It precisely states that he is not directly responsible for the final inputs made by the subject matter experts. It also underlines the fact that he is not responsible for the final quality of the schedule, including logic errors, durations, resource assignments, and other components.

This section is designed to make the recipient understand that ultimately, the result of SQRA depends heavily on the inputs of subject matter experts (SMEs). The analyst is a facilitator and balancing force. He can influence the SMEs by citing facts and approaches, but has no power to change any input values on his own.

Slide 16: Disclaimer-Schedule Integrity

The analyst is not in the position to challenge or revise the schedule, although he did provide opinions and suggestions from a reviewer's perspective. He can't be held responsible for schedule logic errors and interdependencies of the final risk analysis model.

It was largely based on the resources' personal opinions based on individual experience. There are no hard recorded historical evidence presented at any time.

Note that bias may skew the results.

In spite of this, the risk analysis result is still valid in the sense that the inputs came from reliable and experienced sources representing all disciplines.

Figure 76 – Slide 16 Analyst Disclaimer

192

39.19   Slide 17 – Errors and Warnings

The errors and warnings page gives an overview of what activities were flagged by the risk analysis tool. It is the notice given by the risk analysis tool when the analyst runs the risk simulation.

It will calculate the inputs against the network backdrop, providing the results or generating either warnings or errors.

As a rule, all errors have to be corrected or else OPRA will not run, nor will it complete its iteration. Warnings, on the other hand, will not stop the tool from completing the quantification process.

Although warnings are not showstoppers when running the application, it is best to review the activity each message is pointing to. In many cases, these warnings flag something that doesn't make sense with the duration ranges.

Warnings and errors are given if data entered may cause unexpected results when the risk analysis is run. Warnings can be ignored and disabled if required.

The selected warnings are saved with each plan (Primavera Risk Analysis Help, 2009).

As you go through the warnings, you have the chance to make changes to the SME values.

 Do not make any change to the duration range unless approved by the person who provided the input. This is important in order for the input data to remain reliable. It is called vetting the data.

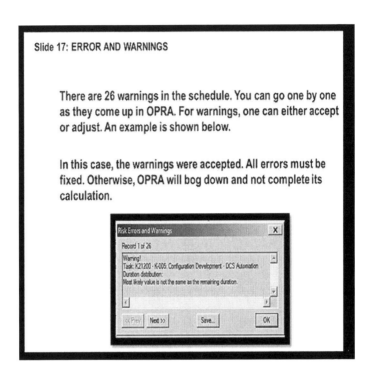

Slide 17: ERROR AND WARNINGS

There are 26 warnings in the schedule. You can go one by one as they come up in OPRA. For warnings, one can either accept or adjust. An example is shown below.

In this case, the warnings were accepted. All errors must be fixed. Otherwise, OPRA will bog down and not complete its calculation.

Figure 77 – Slide 17 Errors and Warnings

Here are some important statements extracted from Section 5.12 of the book *Risk-based Management in the World of Threats and Opportunities: A Project Controls Perspective* on the subject of ranging.

> A subject matter resource who inputs a value that has ML=MIN is trying to say that the remaining duration is flawed and does not represent the expected value of P50.
>
> When he brings the minimum value to equal the most likely value, he is saying that finishing the activity on time using the remaining duration has

less probability.

It will be a bigger challenge than when the ML stays as is, and the minimum value opens up to the left of any specific duration range.

He thinks that the remaining duration of the activity is the earliest possible duration. As such, the remaining duration of the activity is actually nowhere near the most likely deterministic duration value.

Conversely, when ML=MAX, it means that there is no way the activity will complete later than what is shown in the remaining duration of the activity.

It can also be interpreted the Most Likely value as too pessimistic and needs to be recalibrated to a lesser value. The facilitator has to clarify from the subject matter experts (SME) the rationale and act accordingly.

By saying so, the project is assuring that the deterministic value is the same as maximum.

Does this make sense? Something is not quite right if one thinks about it for a moment.

If two of the three values were equal, would it still be a three-point range? What is a good perspective? Are we going to allow this?

If yes, why should we allow this?

Many risk analysts still consider the right triangle distribution as a valid distribution.

Fortunately, the SQRA tool can successfully do the calculation. In other words, there is technically no problem.

> The facilitator should try to avoid such a distribution scenario because it is not a good reflection of the possible ranges and can be self-defeating.

> Such distribution is unrealistic and impossible. The calculation will come out as error. Calculation will stop.

The Most Likely value lying outside the confines of minimum and maximum values is unacceptable.

Calculation will not proceed unless the issue fixed.

> Calculation stops because values relationships do not make sense.

> "When the Most Likely duration equals the, the warning message comes up. This kind of entry is the same as no entry at all if Remaining Duration is equal to Most Likely or RD=ML (Suggestion: Review Section 11)."

> Since there is no duration range provided, it has practically no input to provide. You can ignore the warnings.

A popular distribution is called the TRIGEN (P10/P90). This is a distribution profile where the minimum represents, for example a P10 and your maximum a P90.

The calculation brings into consideration what risk practitioners call "outliers", values which describes the remaining 10% outside the P10/P90 points.

When a subject matter expert provides duration input ranges based on their experience, the assumption considered is that their minimum and maximum value inputs are not true reflections of the actual minimum and maximum.

Rationale:

Even the experts have not experienced the real minimum and maximum values in each of their lifetime.

To compensate for the blind spot, we opt for P10/P90 to consider outliers.

39.20   Slides 18-19 – Probability Distribution

To introduce this major section, a partition cover is suggested. It ushers the readers to the next page containing the schedule quantitative distribution chart.

The distribution chart has the probability calculation results covering all of the project's most important milestones and activities.

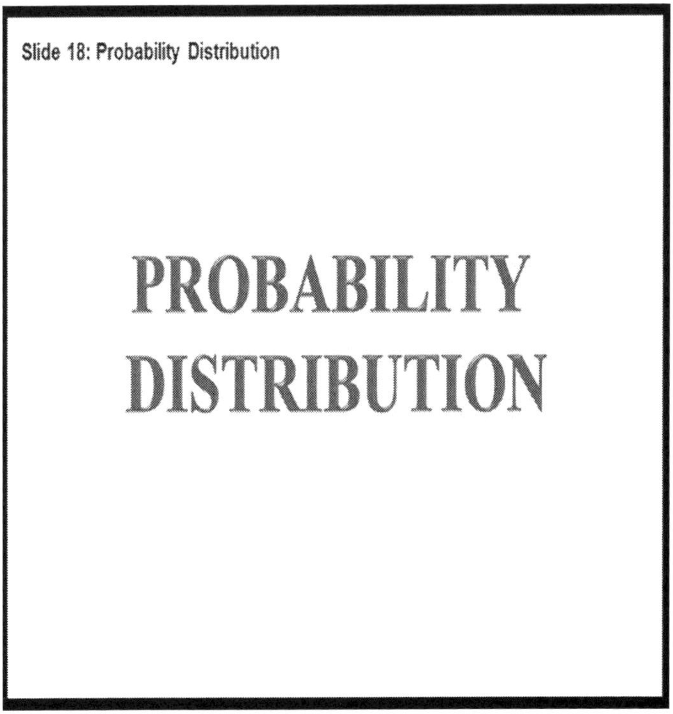

Slide 18: Probability Distribution

PROBABILITY
DISTRIBUTION

Figure 78 – Slide 18 Probability Distribution

If someone wants to know the probability of construction completion or the final turnover milestone, the analyst simply highlights the milestone on the left wing of the distribution window, clicks on it, and captures the information to be placed in the report.

The final turnover is important because it marks the transfer of responsibility from construction management to operation. This last activity of construction represents the end of all construction budgetary allocation. It is the last deliverable, a point when the facility changes hands from the construction group to the commissioning group.

In the case of Project ABC, the last and biggest milestone was KMS1130, described as "First Oil."

The probability distribution of First Oil shows the relationship between probabilities (underlining the level of confidence), and the corresponding dates.

This includes immediate assessment of Project ABC's overall deterministic date (Figure 79 close-up statistics).

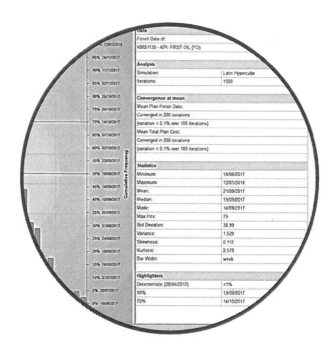

Figure 79 – Slide 19 KMS 1130 (Close-up)

Figure 80 dedicates a whole page to this focal milestone.

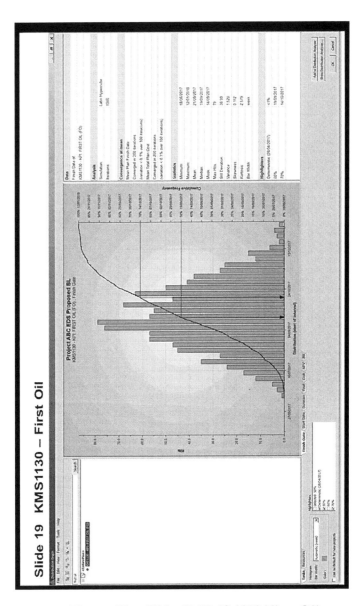

Figure 80 – Slide 19 KMS 1130 First Oil

200

39.21 Slide 20 – Tornado Charts

A tornado chart in SQRA is a form of bar charting where data categories are listed vertically instead of horizontally, presented in the order of largest (top of the chart) down to the smallest (bottom of the chart).

When viewed, they looked like the shape of a tornado or half a tornado.

To introduce this major section, a partition cover is suggested. It ushers the readers to the next page containing the schedule drivers.

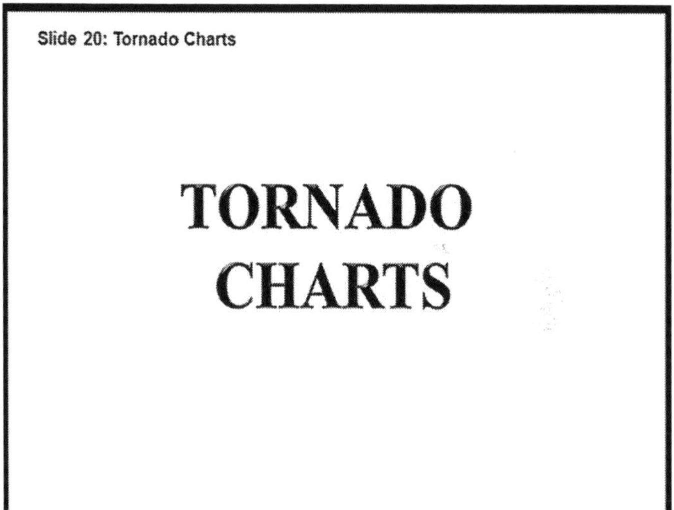

Slide 20: Tornado Charts

TORNADO CHARTS

Figure 81 – Slide 20 Tornado Chart

There are various ways of coming up with the tornado charts, dictated by what method is used. The example illustrations in this Lesson resulted from the traditional method of quantification (three-point range).

The tornado chart has five optional views in OPRA.

Duration Sensitivity
Cost Sensitivity (for cost-loaded schedules only).
We will skip this in our discussion.
Criticality Index
Cruciality
Schedule Sensitivity Index

39.22   Slide 20.1 Duration Sensitivity

Let us discuss duration sensitivity together (Figure 82). Duration sensitivity is a measure of the correlation between the duration of a work activity and the duration of the project.

"It gives a hint of how much the duration of each activity influences completion of other activities or the entire project. It can be used for identifying tasks that are most likely to cause delay or increase the duration of a project.

The sensitivity values for each work activity can be viewed in a Gantt Chart column or in the Tornado Graph.

The schedule activity with the highest duration sensitivity is the task that will most likely increase the overall project duration.

Sensitivity ranges from -100% to +100% (OPRA, 2009. e-Help User Manual)"

The chart shows the sensitivity of the project to duration changes of the top ten listed activities.

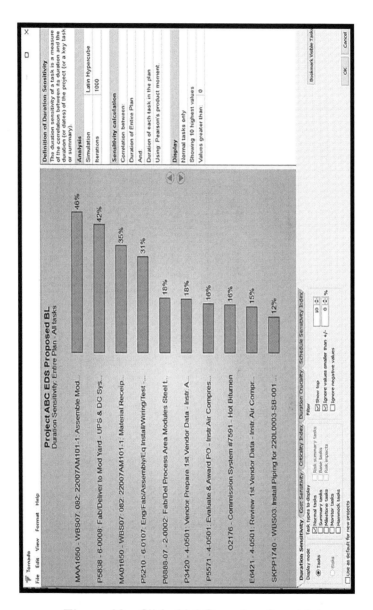

Figure 82 – Slide 20.1 Duration Sensitivity

Managing these activities is the best opportunity to reduce overall duration compared to all the other activities in the schedule. You can start with the top four activities, though focusing on the rest of the activities will provide an even better result. On many occasions, it is a question of time.

One must bear in mind that the greater the duration involved, the greater the sensitivity and chance of pushing the schedule out. If the activities lie on the same logical path, improving even just one activity can release the others. Activities found in the other tornado charts confirm their greater influence to affect and alter the end date.

39.23   Slide 20.2 Criticality Index

Listed in Figure 83 were 30 critical activities from about 140 critical tasks identified by OPRA. This represents about 21% of the total number of critical activities in the remaining schedule. These critical activities will require attention.

The Paretto principle says that by addressing the top 20% of the critical issues, one will solve the remaining 80%. We can quickly say, therefore, that the 30 activities highlighted present us the opportunity to use that concept.

This criticality index represents the dynamic path and allows us to identify the tasks that are likely to cause delays more objectively (OPRA, 2009. Help). By monitoring tasks with a high criticality index, a project is less likely to be late. The index is calculated after a quantitative risk analysis. It is the percentage of time a task stays on the critical path during analysis. If a task has an 83% criticality index, like Activity ID: SST1870 Set Module: Pipe way/Cable trays, it means that during the 1000 iterations, the critical path included the task 83% of the time. The task is therefore likely to be key to completing the project on time. Conversely, tasks with a low criticality index are much less likely to cause a delay in the project finish date.

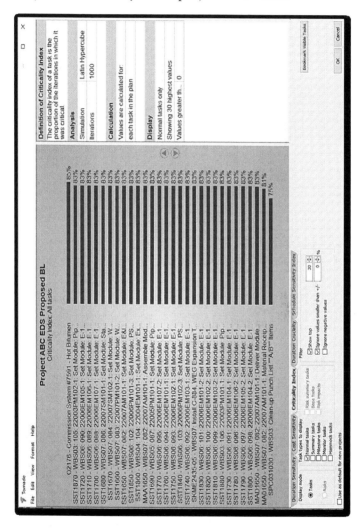

Figure 83 – Slide 20.2 Criticality Index

39.24   Slide 20.3 Cruciality

Cruciality (Figure 84) was calculated from the duration sensitivity and the criticality index. It is an indicator of where to best spend time on mitigating or further defining schedule durations and logic, as it is a function of how many times the activity is on the critical path and how sensitive the end date is to that activity.

Note that several activities highlighted in the criticality index were also found on the cruciality list.

An ongoing review of schedule logic quality and close monitoring of progress on the indicated activities should be carried out throughout the life of the project.

> "Cruciality is calculated from the Duration Sensitivity and the Criticality index.
>
> Cruciality = Duration Sensitivity x Criticality index
>
> Duration Sensitivity can display low positive and negative values for activities that are not on the critical path. High sensitivity are red flags requiring attention.
>
> Low values are due to random correlation between the task and the project duration.
>
> These low positive and negative values for Duration Sensitivity can be filtered out by selecting only Duration Sensitivity values greater than a specified value in the Tornado Chart (Source: OPRA, 2009. Help)."

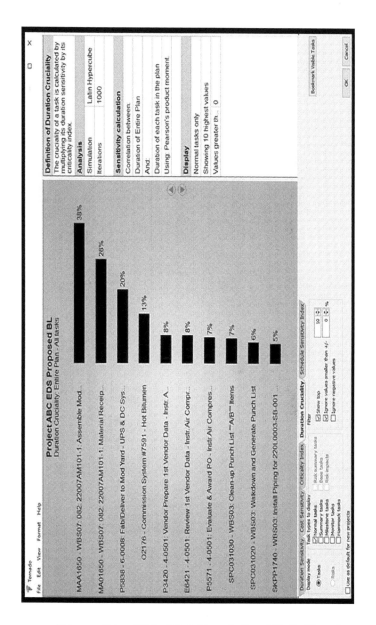

Figure 84 – Slide 20.3 Cruciality (Full Chart)

207

39.25   Slide 20.4 Schedule Sensitivity Index (SSI)

The SSI (Figure 85) identifies and ranks the tasks most likely to influence the project duration and finish date (OPRA, 2009. Help). SSI is expressed as a percentage using the following calculation:

$$SSI = \frac{(Criticality\ index)(Task\ Standard\ Deviation)}{(Project\ Standard\ Deviation)}$$

Combining criticality with the task standard deviation gives the highest values to tasks that are on the critical path and have a large range of uncertainty.

This overcomes the fact that criticality takes no account of uncertainty on an individual task, and consequently a task with no uncertainty can still have 100% criticality.

The project standard deviation is likely to be larger than any individual task's standard deviation.

If a task dominates a schedule's uncertainty, its SSI will tend towards 100%.

The project team should look closely to determine whether the activities listed have real issues in them needing to be resolved. The project team must address the top four activities on the list. If any of the four lie on the same critical path, the greater the possible improvement. Mitigating one, will improve the criticality of the other activities, and overall critical path.

For example: MAA1650 Assemble Module is in the same logical chain as MAD1650. Improving one of them practically improves the second activity, and the activities that lie on the same path.

208

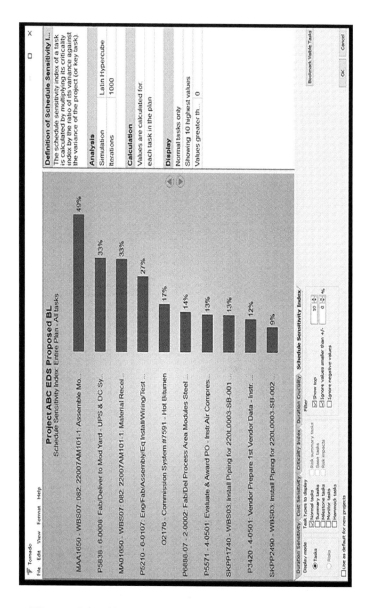

Figure 85 – Slide 20.4 Schedule Sensitivity Index

209

If the associated risks for activities belonging to the same logic chain are the same, only one activity should be ranged. Otherwise, the central limit theorem can cancel out the true impact.

Another thing is the issue attributed with excessive lags. We have identified that 37% of all relationships in the schedule have lags, or 3286 relationships. 432 of these activities have a lag of more than 15 days. These are relationships that might be unnecessarily driving other activities. Managing these types of relationships is difficult.

It is also wise to review activities with SS or FF relationship that have relatively excessive lags (i.e. lags of more than 3-months) and breaking down some parts of the schedule to make these more manageable.

39.26   Slide 21 – Criticality Distribution Profile

This distribution profile (Figure 86) plots the spread of the criticality index (OPRA, 2009. Help) in Project ABC and provides an indication of the number activities threatening to delay the project.

These are activities on paths that reside on or near the primary critical path.

The criticality distribution profile summarizes the number of activities whose criticality falls within various limits up to 100% (ibid).

It is a measure of network flexibility and tightness.

By knowing the number of critical activities in the schedule and how critical they are, the project can act in a timely manner.

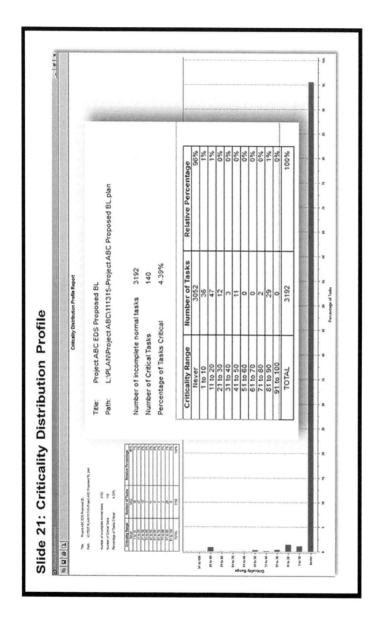

Figure 86 – Slide 21 Criticality Distribution Profile

211

If the percentage of activities that are critical goes beyond 50%, the project schedule is relatively tight.

Project ABC is quite flexible, with the percentage of critical tasks equal to only 4.39% only. This is good news for the project.

A very tight schedule cannot offer much room for adjustment. When one critical path primary driver is addressed and mitigated, the criticality will be transferred to another.

The distribution of criticality was not significant in Project ABC. It was low.

The network is not tight because it shows a relatively low number of activities with criticality between 20 and 100 percent. About 96% of network activities were never on the critical path.

39.27   Slide 22 – Criticality Path Report

The risk analysis tool examines the criticality of predecessor activities in each branch from a focal activity and calculates back to the start of the network. The focal activity can be an end-deliverable milestone or an activity elsewhere in the network.

> "The Criticality Path Report creates a report on the path throughout the integrated project containing the activities with the highest criticality index values. Any delay to a 100 percent critical activity will have a direct impact on the overall project completion date. The number of days the activity is delayed equals the number of days the completion date is delayed.

Slide 22: Criticality Path Report

Criticality Path Report

Task Status: *Completed* +Underway+

Criticality Path

Name	Description	Rem Dur	Criticality
E26239	4-0501: Prep/Issue Technical RFQ Pkg to Procurement -	10	17.90%
P25826	4-0501: Prep/Issue RFQ Pkg - Instr.Air Compressor Pkg	10	17.90%
P25336	4-0501: Bid Period - Instr.Air Compressor Pkg - Re-bid	20	17.90%
E6418	4-0501: Technical Bid Evaluation - Instr. Air Compressor	40	22.10%
E6419	4-0501: MR Request for PO - Instr. Air Compressor Pkg (	9	22.10%
P5571	4-0501: Evaluate & Award PO - Instr.Air Compressor Pk(	67	43.90%
P3420	4-0501: Vendor Prepare 1st Vendor Data - Instr. Air Corr	26	43.90%
E6421	4-0501: Review 1st Vendor Data - Instr. Air Compressor	10	50.50%
EEL1145	Update & Issue Electrical UPS Load List - IFD	27	49.20%

Figure 87 – Slide 22 Criticality Path Report

The selection depends on how important the activity is to the project. OPRA's default sequence for the printed report has it from the start to the end activity of a network.

The criticality path report (Figure 87) is a tabulated list of the schedule network path, indicating the criticality index value of each activity (OPRA, 2009. Help)."

Percent criticality represents the probability of an activity being on the critical path during project execution. It also points to the relative importance of one activity over others in the network.

39.28 Slide 22 – Distribution Analyzer

The Distribution Analyzer (Figure 88) records the S-curve of each activity data point that the project would like to focus on in the Distribution Chart window. The probability distribution of any activity in the form of an S-curve can be generated in the Distribution Analyzer window and saved. This allows the analyst to compare the curves and histograms of activities for selected projects, enabling a useful and quick comparison.

The S-curve from the data imported becomes a static record after import. It has no more links to the live data. Updating the PLAN file and re-running the quantification process will not update the saved distribution profile. The multi-modal peaks (M1-M5) are indication of schedule calendar impacts. These represent opportunities, a chance for the team to come up with better execution calendars, which can allow more activities to complete earlier or on time.

The way the contractor manages the schedule calendar limits the more effective adjustment of these peaks and gaps. The project should pursue any possible improvements relevant to addressing these peaks. The project has a chance to appreciate the cumulative and non-cumulative probability distribution versus the activity dates corresponding to each point on the S-curve. A number of project control professionals prefer to use the Distribution Analyzer as their centerpiece when presenting schedule contingency to upper management because of the comparison capability and the uncluttered view, which seems to offer an easier to understand form.

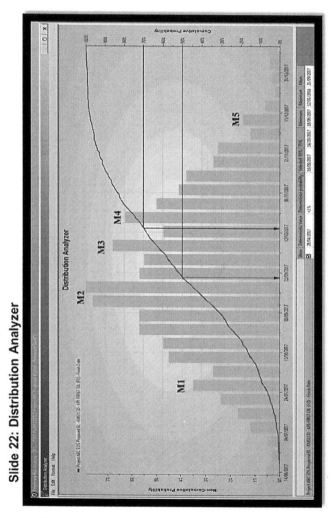

Figure 88 – Slide 22 Distribution Analyzer

39.29   Slides 23-24 – Progress Curve & Histogram

One of the methods available to the project is the review of the project's construction progress curve and histogram (Figure 89). A good planner/scheduler can generate this chart relatively quickly if the schedule has already been resource-loaded.

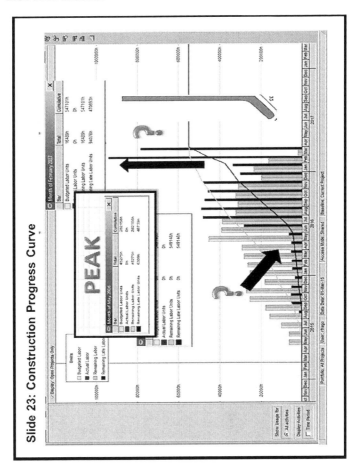

Figure 89 – Slide 23 Construction Progress Chart

Inspection of the construction progress curve and histogram can provide useful risk indicators. Knowing them will provide insights on aspects of the schedule that are usually hidden from view. It gives a good handle to the project. Useful risk indicators (see Figure 89 and Figure 90):

Schedule alignment with the frozen estimate
Schedule flexibility
Schedule achievability
Schedule peaks and lows
Schedule soundness
Schedule accuracy

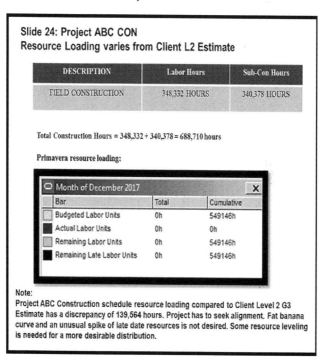

Figure 90 – Slide 24 Loading not aligned to Estimate

The resource loading of Project ABC's schedule was not accurate. Compared to the approved estimate, the loaded total work hours used for progressing has a discrepancy of 139,564 hours. This kind of misalignment is unacceptable.

Project ABC has to seek alignment in order for the progress curve and histogram to be useful in forecasting.

In spite of this missing information, the available data has already produced a fat banana curve, including an unusual spike in late date resources. This is not desired.

The planner/scheduler has to level the resources to come up with a more desirable distribution.

39.30   Slides 25-26 – Labor Density and Complexity

Labor density is equal to the total effective construction work area per worker. The formula is based on the maximum/economic total number of crafts/laborers working at peak (supervision not included). It was based on historical experience (Bent, 1996).

The size of the work area is directly related to the number of crafts/laborers. As the work area decreases, the number of people who can work in the area also decreases.

Complexity is inversely related to the number of crafts/laborers who can work in a construction area; i.e. direct man-hours per square feet.

This means that as the complexity of the area increases, the number of people who can work in that particular area decreases. A project involving more capital equipment has

218

greater complexity and more labor hours. The presence of equipment takes up space in which people could otherwise work (ibid).

 The widely accepted labor density and complexity benchmarks are 180 to 200 square feet per person and 4 to 5 workhours per square foot for an average unit (ibid). Use these indicators to evaluate the soundness of the schedule in terms of safety and achievability.

In the process of digging deeper into the subject of labor density and complexity, I reached out to the author/developer of the Fast Track Trapezoidal Technique (FTTT) method of forecasting project durations, Mr. James Bent. Labor density and complexity is closely tied to his FTTT calculations.

Mr. Bent developed the FTTT conceptual estimating formula for forecasting project schedule durations some three decades ago.

In our correspondence, he mentioned that it took him only a couple of years to find that the answers were amazingly accurate if the correct complexity and density factors were utilized.

The basis of his research was a period of 25 years covering project performances from 1975 to 1990. Although there were major advancements in technology, machineries, designs, communications, tools, and techniques from 1990 to the present, the author claims that the FTTT calculation concept is applicable with today's projects.

This should only be applied to work from the first start of construction. It was used on re-vamp projects, but only very carefully and with limited success. The advancement of new construction techniques and design elements is covered by the conceptual range of the factors. To date, I have not come across any contradictory information or data. This was confirmed by Mr. Bent.

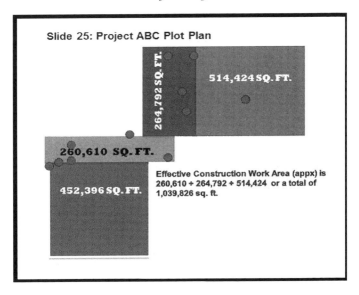

Figure 91 – Slide 25 Work Area Plot Plan

When calculating labor density, and complexity, the effective work area has to be calculated. To do this, one has to understand its basis. The effective construction work area is the area bounded by the battery limits of the complete units where there has been no allowance for future expansion. It is the area where there is normal grouping of equipment at ground level or equipment structures, according to economic design and construction parameters but not for modular construction.

Jamie added that the FTTT formula would not apply to Middle East projects, as economic ground layouts are rarely the case. Land is cheap compared to the West. In such cases, and if the work is not a complete process unit, the area data is determined by adding some three (3) to five (5) meters to the outside of the equipment placement area.

Slide 26: Labor Density and Complexity

Reference Table:
FT/TT Conceptual Estimating   by J. Bent

CONSTRUCTION COMPLEXITY & LABOR DENSITY
●● Only applicable to "complete" Process Units (small or large)
●● Assumes an economic design environment
●● Based on "average" US labor productivity (Calif./Union)

COMPLEXITY (direct manhours/sq. ft.)

	Manhours/sq ft.
SIMPLE UNIT	4/5
AVERAGE UNIT	6/7 } x 2
COMPLEX UNIT	8/10
PROCESS MODULES	

LABOR DENSITY (sq. ft./man)
Tied to above Complexity Data

	Sq. ft./man
SIMPLE UNIT (4/5 mh./sq. ft.)	150/180
AVERAGE UNIT (6/7 mn./sq. ft.)	180/250
COMPLEX UNIT (8/10 mn./sq. ft.)	250/300
*PROCESS*G* MODULES	180/200

Item No.	A) Description	B) INPUT	C) Calculated Value	D) REMARKS
1	PROJECT ABC Q3			
2	Cross-sectional Area (PROJECT ABC) in SQ. FT	1,032,826		Area in close proximity to the equipment. Involves only areas contributing to the peak labor hours.
3	Complexity from Guidelines, Hours per SQ. FT	5		AVERAGE complexity benchmark = 5. Total Direct workhours per SQ. FT. The lower the PF, the greater the estimated hours, i.e. PF=Planned/Actual
4	Assumed Project's Average P.f. (0.6)	0.6		
5	Direct Labour hours (Scope)		549,149.0	From Primavera
6	Direct Labour hours (Scope)		988,710.0	From the Frozen Estimate
7	Peak Labour Hours (will occur in May 2015)	45,275		
8	Peak Labor (Total)		209	
9	Standard Work Week in hours @10-4, 10 Hours per day calendar	50		
10	Effective Workhours per month		217	
11	Labor Density Assumed in SQ.FT per worker		4,926	Project has enough safe area to work in.

Above result indicates that there is no danger to personnel safety. There is more than enough lot area to work in. No foreseen adverse effect to typical productivity value.

Figure 92 – Slide 26 Labor Density and Complexity

Let us go back to the sample Project ABC. The project engineer has calculated the total effective construction work area to be 1,039,826 square feet (Figure 92).

The planner/scheduler reported a resource peak of 45,725 workhours (Figure 89). The peak labor value in terms of direct workhours was generated from the Primavera scheduling tool.

The workhours have to be converted to a peak equivalent workforce either by calculation or directly from the produced schedule histogram.

With the two values known, labor density and complexity can be calculated. Using the FTTT density and complexity benchmarks of 200 and 5, the results show that the project is not too complex, with more than enough total work area for workers to safely work in.

$$Labour\ density = \frac{1,039,826\ sq.ft.}{45,725\ hours\ \left(\frac{1\ worker}{217\ hours}\right)}$$

$$= 4,976\ sq.ft.per\ worker$$

Since 4,976 > 200, the work area is safe and sufficient to work in.

$$Complexity = \frac{688,710\ workhours}{1,039,826\ sq.ft.}$$

$$= 0.66\ workhours\ per\ sq.ft.$$

Since 0.66 < 5, construction work complexity is well within the acceptable benchmark.

Make sure that the resource loading of the schedule is equal to the approved estimate. In this example, the labor density was calculated based on the loading that still has a discrepancy of 139,564 hours. The loading must be corrected, and the resource peak generated once more.

Once the loading is corrected, do another calculation using the peak value generated by the scheduling tool. The peak will probably change slightly, or significantly, depending on how the variance value is loaded.

Will FTTT work on other industrial work setup? Take for example the mining industry where the site battery limits is huge. Of course it will and for obvious reason.

The bigger work space the project has, the lower the labor density becomes, and the safer it is to work. In spite of this expectation, one should not let his guards down because there are other reasons affecting workplace safety.

The project must strive to use the correct data for these calculations.

39.31   Recommendation

To improve the probability of achieving the key deliverables in this schedule, the analyst has to provide some direction for the project. The recommendations for the project can be a separate report or incorporated as the last slide. Project ABC received the following recommendations:

- Identify those schedule drivers sitting on the same logic path and address them.

- Ensure complete alignment of the dates identified on the Key Performance Milestone before finalizing the Project ABC contract.

- Complete the risk analysis of the most current (updated) schedule before agreeing to a contract baseline. Some of the same risk inputs can be used for the remaining activities.
- Identify activities with extremely long durations and break them down to a more manageable level, if possible, to acquire more control.

- Long duration activities carry more risks with them. The project's overall duration is very sensitive to such activities. Evaluate work efforts associated with long duration, critical activities.

- Ensure complete alignment of the Module/Fabrication, Construction, and C&SU schedule.

- Include PSSR (Pre-Startup Safety Review) and Closeout activities in the schedule. PSSR is a safety review conducted before commissioning and start-up to make sure that installations meet the design or operating intent, to catch and re-assess any potential hazard due to changes during the detailed engineering and construction phase of a project. The project wants to make sure that

224

the facility os "Ready for Start-up (PSSR, 2019)."

- Recheck the integrated approach between contractors, and clients. Discuss proper control of work access early.

- Control planning and interface management tightly.

- Once the project officially settles on a firm restart date, it would be beneficial to do another review of the schedule logic and duration, incorporate mitigation in the schedule, and run another SQRA.

- Re-assess Project ABC's schedule drivers when the risk actions are effectively taken and issued for implementation.

- Monitor and record how close KPI Milestones are to subsequent actuals. This will be very good benchmarking information.

- Choose the most appropriate risk reduction strategy to reach the lowest residual risk level.

- Carefully allocate resources to the dynamic schedule drivers, making every effort to expedite completion while achieving all planned objectives.

- Perform realistic but optimized leads and lags

adjustment. Bear in mind that improper use of leads and lags can distort a schedule.

- Filter all activities with excessive total float and identify the opportunities they offer in accommodating activities in the free float zone.

- The planning team should revisit the existing FF relationships in the schedule. There are an excessive number of Finish-to-finish (parallel) relationships. That accounts for 37% of all relationships, equivalent to 3,259 links.

- Check if this can be improved, bearing in mind that FF links introduce more risks towards the end, when the remaining activities tend to line up together, bringing big challenges to resources and resource management.

- Excessive FF relationships produce the hockey stick shaped resource histogram.

- Conduct another risk analysis to validate the final baseline. Ensure that SQRA is performed no more than a week from the data date. If certain activities after the data date are already completed during quantification, they should sit on the right dates but not be actualized.

- Use a SWOT structured analysis to evaluate

the strengths, weaknesses, opportunities, and
threats involved in schedule management as
required, and revisit this on a periodic basis.

- Focus upstream. Good risk preparation
  upstream prevents many liabilities
  downstream.

40. What You Have Learned

This book is fundamentally a summary for anyone who wants to try another approach to effective schedule baselining.

Not only did we touch on the qualitative aspect of schedule management, you have also looked closer to schedule quantification.

This is improving your knowledge and skills to good measure!

The author used a non-rigid, non-academic approach in the discussion of topics from the scheduling concepts and philosophies of schedule baseline development based on today's growing trend, developing not just a schedule but a risk-based schedule.

The same conversational approach hopes to provide impetus to learning. This is the time to share such knowledge to those professionals who are interested in doing a much better job to schedule baseline creation, development and management.

Section 1 and 2 introduced the reader to the world of schedule risk-based management. Your real-life previous experience was called upon and learning comes easy. You were surprised that you've understood more than what you've expected, reading just a few pages.

Section 3 provided a brief summary of the schedule

quantitative risk analysis process. It became clear that it is a process that calculates overall probability or chance of completing a project on time and on budget.

Section 4 to 6 offered everyone a better understanding of risk and risk-based management through visualization while Section 7 to 9 touches on what risk-simulation is about, the popular tools/techniques being used, and the advantage of doing schedule quantitative risk analysis.

Project contingency, duration ranging using the three point estimate, and the importance of good data quality were lively discussed in Section 10 to 13. You learned that duration ranging using three-point estimating is referred to as the 'traditional method of quantification."

Validating the project schedule as an essential prerequisite prior to full-fledged SQRA was tackled in Section 14. The bottom-line emphasis was short and simple, and that is, "The schedule must be the right sample." Good schedule quality is the decent starting point of every schedule risk quantification.

Section 15 to 18 delves deeper into essential attributes affecting risk analysis, such as calendars, quality of the proposed schedule baselines, the use of filters, and your understanding of the static path.

Many planners/schedulers do not take good care of their schedule calendars. They take on a new project schedule without inspecting the attributes of the assigned calendars. Sometimes, the calendar runs short, the attributes of which was not specified up to the duration of the project. Error in calendar assignments makes progress and duration calculation erroneous. The wrong calendar affects all the activities that should have had a different calendar.

You learned that Baseline Schedules should never be developed and built in isolation. It should have the inputs of all stakeholders and must represent the "most likely" duration with no built-in risk.

Isn't it nice to appreciate that the critical path identified by your P6 application derived from the deterministic schedule are static critical path? It means they were but a snapshot of the path in time.

The vital significance of an integrated analysis was specially mentioned in Section 19, followed by a comprehensive dissertation of various approaches to schedule risk modeling (Section 20 to 23).

Review these sections so you can weigh in into the debates that are still going on in the profession and enjoy the intellectual discourse at the same time.

Section 24 gave the necessary relational perspective between contracts and schedules. You realized that regardless of how much detailed information the project has, the contract will dictate its control level. If it prescribed Level 3 control schedule, then it has to be.

What should really be the optimum size of the schedule model for risk analysis? If you've gone through Section 25, you already know the answer. The practicality of running SQRA using the detailed schedule was underlined in this section.

OPRA as a risk analysis tool has no limitation to what it can handle. Running a project portfolio as large as 15,000 to 50,000 activities is not a problem.

Section 26 highlighted the growing number of risk managers who believe that the ideal method is an integrated cost and schedule quantitative risk analysis (ICSQRA).

Medium-size projects to mega should find a way to unite the cost-schedule components to get the complete picture. Doing them separately creates informational gaps.

The challenge of political dates imposed on a schedule was an interesting subject in Section 27, resulting in an important question. Which model to use (Section 28)?

Section 29 to 38 were excellent guiding posts to SQRA from initial engagement, preparation, identifying participants, modeling philosophy, and ranging.

You learned several tips on how to avoid the snares of double-dipping and other sticking points.

The excellent thing about this is the author taught you how to fix the issues. Knowing what to do will separate you from the others.

A comprehensive schedule quantitative risk analysis reporting job aids comprise Section 39 and its cover to cover sub-sections (39.1 to 39.31).

The would-be analyst will find them very useful in coming up with own professional style of conveying information. I hope they've helped you too.

Bibliography

1.1. Frago, R. (July-2013).Schedule Quantitative Risk Assessment (SQRA) Fundamentals: Using Three Point Estimate.Slideshare.com.Retrieved from http://www.slideshare.net/rfrago/071613-introduction-to-sqra-traditional-method

1.2. Frago, R. (July-2013).How to Prepare for Schedule Quantitative Risk Assessment.Slideshare.com.Retrieved from http://www.slideshare.net/rfrago/071513-how-to-prepare-for-sqra-by-rcf

1.3. Oracle University (2011).Managing Risk in Oracle Primavera Risk Analysis.Versions 6.0/6.1 Course Manual

1.4. PRC Software Website (2013).Primavera Risk: Step 2 – Pertmaster Import Check.Retrieved from http://www.prcsoftware.com/product-primavera-risk-pertmaster-training/41-pertmaster-step-2-import-validation.html

1.5. Planning Planet blogs (2011).P6 XER Imported into PertMaster 8 Resulted into Different Dates.Planning Planet Forum.Retrieved from http://www.planningplanet.com/forums/schedule-risk-and-schedule-risk-analysis/499990/please-help-asapp6-xer-imported-pertmaster-8-

1.6.   PMSite blogs (2013).Importing From P6 to PertMaster.Thread.Retrieved from http://pmsite.com/forums/viewthread/1624/

1.7.   Wicklund, A. (Sep-2013). Youtube:Primavera Risk (Pertmaster) - Step 1 - P6 Database Import.Youtube.com.Retrieved from http://www.youtube.com/watch?v=jIq1xjZ6_io

1.8.   Wicklund, A. (Sep-2013). Youtube: Primavera Risk (Pertmaster) - Step 2 - Import Check Tab.Youtube.com.Retrieved from http://www.youtube.com/watch?v=jIq1xjZ6_io

Additional Reading

Frago, R., (2015).Risk-based Management in the World of Threats and Opportunities: A Project Controls Standard. ISBN 978-0-9947608-0-7 (Canada)

Frago, R., (2015).Plan to Schedule, Schedule to Plan. ISBN 978-0-9947608-2-1 (Canada)

Frago, R., (2015).How to Create a Good Quality Risk-based Baseline Schedule. ISBN 978-0-9947608-1-4 (Canada)

Acronyms

AACE	Association for the Advancement of Cost Engineering
ALAP	As late as possible constraint
BL	Baseline
BOS	Basis of schedule
CLT	Central Limit Theorem
CP	Critical path
CPM	Critical path method
EDS	Engineering Design Specification
FF	Finish to Finish
FS	Finish to Start
GIGO	Garbage in, Garbage out
L/A	Links to activity ratio
LDT	Line designation table
LH	Latin Hypercube
LOE	Level of Effort
MAX	Maximum or Pessimistic
MIN	Minimum or Optimistic
ML	Most Likely

MS	Milestones
MSP	Microsoft Projects
MSQ	Minimum Schedule Quality
OPRA	Oracle Primavera Risk Analysis (previously Pertmaster)
P50	50% Probability
PM	Project Management
PMBOK	Project Management Body of Knowledge
PMI	Project Management Institute
PPM	Project Portfolio Management
RBM	Risk-based Management
RD	Remaining Duration
RI	Redundancy Index
RMP	Risk Management Professional
SF	Start to Finish
SQRA	Schedule Quantitative Risk Analysis
SS	Start to Start
TF	Total Float
ZFF	Zero Free Float

INDEX

adjustment to the import setting 132

Analysis tab 141

availability of time 68

baseline 51

benchmark criteria 42

Changing Triangle to Trigen 165

computer jockeys 77

control schedule 187

converted three-point range.. 132

deal with the multiple calendars.. 134

Deltek-Acumen Fuse..42

details 71

deterministic date 130

disclaimer page 192

Distribution Analyzer.. 150

distribution chart..29

Distribution Chart..88

Distribution Charts 146

double-dipping 37

Duration ranging..31

errors and warnings page.. 193

filter the schedule's critical..53

First Oil.. 184

fly above the forest...71

Garbage in, Garbage out.. 121

Go or No Go.. 118

ICSQRA 81

if the data quality is poor 131

import mapping dialog box... 135

import will generate a log 125

Inexperience..65

Input Sheet...92

iteration...74, 140

iterations 20

key performance milestones... 169
Lags and leads calculation.. 130
large model..79
main objective..68
Monte Carlo..19
multiple calendars 124
one risk model..81
OPRA schedule check... 190
optimum schedule size..77
Options button... 140
Original Deterministic dates 138
overall probability 7
Planning Unit... 146
population 171
Primary data.. 171
Process-centric..78
quality analyzer tools 188
quality assessment tools...42
quality of planning data.. 121
quality of the schedule...70
ranges 144
Re-creating a schedule..68
relevant risks 38
risk factors..53
Risk Register 31
Risk scoring..31
risk session...32
schedule owner...75
Schedule Quantitative Risk Analysis (SQRA) 119
secondary critical path..61
snapshot...55
SQRA...5, 39, 169
SQRA Report Format... 167
standard 8-hour per day... 130
Start and Finish Dates... 138
strategic objective...71
summarized schedule model 61

three-point range... 132
three-point values.. 125
transfer of responsibility 198
translation... 132
trigger 51
UDF 5
User 5
Warnings... 142
XER 92

About the Author

Rufran C. Frago P. Eng., PMP, CCP, PMI-RMP is the CEO and Founder of PM Solution Pro and KATHAKO, two of Calgary's consulting, product, and training tradenames operating under Risk-based Management and Services Inc., focusing on project/business management best practice and creative solution. He is passionate in providing advice and education through expert consultation, collaboration, and what he uniquely calls, student-led (client-led) training.

Mr. Frago has more than four decades of international work experience in Nuclear/Utilities, Oil & Gas, Petrochemicals, Oleo-chemicals, Sugar Refining, Manufacturing, Consulting, and Education. He worked with known multinational companies in various parts of the world like Asia, Middle East, Canada, and North Africa. Rufran has worked with Caltex, Uniman, Unichem (now Cocochem), ARAMCO-KSA, Central Azucarera de Tarlac, Arabian Gulf Oil Company-Libya, Batangas State University, Saint Bridget's College, JG Summit Petrochemicals, Halliburton-Kellogg, Brown and Root, OPTI Canada, Suncor Energy Inc., Bruce Power, and Burns & McDonnell.

His expertise includes risk-based management, risk analysis, planning & scheduling, cost management, project controls, project integration, auditing, maintenance, operation, material selection, warehousing, EH&S and reliability engineering. He is interested in providing solutions and innovations to all clients and stakeholders.

He is passionate about teaching and mentoring, designing the ZERO P6, ZERO FUSE, and ZERO OPRA curriculum for self-start beginners, future management practitioners who have not used the aforementioned tools before or have no idea of their practical use.

These five-hours courses offer a focused, one-on-one engagement he proudly calls "student-led learning," strongly believing that this more personal and collaborative approach shall satisfy all of the student goals.

Rufran authored the books - *Risk-based Management in the World of Threats and Opportunities ISBN 978-0-9947608-0-7, How to Create a Good P50 Risk-based Baseline Schedule ISBN 978-0-9947608-1-4, and Plan to Schedule, Schedule to Plan ISBN 978-0-9947608-2-1.*

Mr. Frago is a Filipino born Canadian risk-based management practitioner. He studied at Batangas State University and University of Batangas graduated with a Diploma in Petroleum Refinery Maintenance Technician (1979), Bachelor of Science in Mechanical Engineering (1984), and Bachelor of Science in Management Engineering in 1987 respectively. He was also an undergraduate of Bachelor of Science in Electrical Engineering needing only one semester to complete.

He continued his education by taking up MBA courses under the University of the Philippines-PBMIT Consortium (1987-1988). Rufran completed Computer Technician Program at International Correspondence School, Pennsylvania, USA in 1994, Applied Project Management Certificate program at Southern Alberta Institute of Technology in 2009, and Professional Management Certificate program specializing in Construction

Management in 2014. He is taking up Professional Management Certificate program specializing in Risk Management at University of Calgary.

He was a recipient of the Gerry Roxas Leadership Award (1976) and the American Field Service (AFS) Scholarship in 1976-77, studying in America for a year. California-Texas Philippines (Caltex Philippines Inc.), one of Asia's biggest oil and gas refineries at the time, awards him with a two-year national college scholarship, specializing in Petroleum Refinery Maintenance.

The author wants to share his knowledge and leave behind some legacy to all readers, and his family, most especially to his wife, children and lovely grandchildren, Eva and Mia.

e-mail: rcfrago@gmail.com

consultant @pmsolutionpro.com

rbms.inc@gmail.com

Author's websites:

https://www.amazon.com/author/rufrancfrago

http://ca.linkedin.com/in/rufranfrago

https://www.facebook.com/pmsolutionpro/

https://pmsolutionpro.com/

https://kathako.com/

Book Announcement!

"Risk-based Management in the World of Threats and Opportunities: A Project Controls Perspective"

ISBN 978-0-9947608-0-7

Risk-based Management in the World of Threats and Opportunities provides new and additional knowledge to project management practitioners, risk management specialists, and for undergraduate students taking up courses in Risk Management.

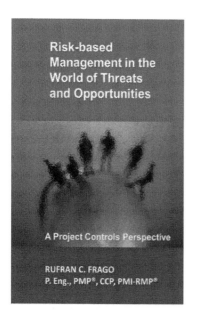

Risk-based Management in the World of Threats and Opportunities

A Project Controls Perspective

RUFRAN C. FRAGO
P. Eng., PMP®, CCP, PMI-RMP®

The purpose of life is managing risk. It is in front of all of us and in the very fabric of our daily life. Risk management is the only thing we do for a living. This is the reason why we go to work every day. If we still do not realize this intriguing conclusion then I guess, we are all familiar with risks like close friends, but we still do not know them well enough.

Grab a copy, read and I will show you how to better appreciate the word risk, threat, opportunity, and the concept of risk-based management in the simplest terms. The sectional contents offer practical and common-sense approach surrounding risk-based thinking to managers, directors, aspiring industry professionals, and newcomers.

The material is especially design to start with the foundational principles and gradually bringing the reader to deeper topics using simple terminologies in conversational style. Risk-based management is a serious approach and a philosophy that takes risk as major consideration while managing any endeavor throughout its life cycle. Risk-based management increases the probability of success in achieving organizational and individual objectives.

It simply means that risk should be the main focus of anyone while keeping an eye to achieving objectives. Risk is a primary concern in pursuit of a goal. Risk is not only a factor or featured element of management. It is the main character at play. Risk-based management gives importance to objectives.

Failing to mitigate the risk means failure to meet the objective/s. Each Lesson is an open-minded appraisal of risk, its concept, its approaches, its visual, basis, assumptions, methodologies, tools, and applications. Risk attributes were revisited and explained in a more vivid, flexible and friendly manner.

The author wants to talk about risk and risk-based management with someone fresh from high school and one deep in the fields yet coming to the same understanding because this book has bridged understanding. One must remember the idea of risk like a picture. If the book manages to accomplish that, then I consider the book a success.

Learn the fundamentals and apply them to whatever you do, from a simple yardwork to managing a $10Billion dollars project.

Available in PM Solution Pro (https://pmsolutionpro.com), Amazon.com, Chapters, Indigo, and various international outlets and bookstores in paperback and e-book.

"Plan to Schedule, Schedule to Plan"
ISBN 978-0-9947608-2-1

This book is for everyone who wants to improve their knowledge and skills in risk-based project time management. The author uses a non-rigid, non-academic approach in the discussion of topics from the concepts and philosophies of planning and scheduling, its development through the Gates, and the various related other processes involved.

Plan to schedule, Schedule to Plan attempts to remedy the brain drain plaguing all related management fields. It provides clear line of sight between risk-based planning and scheduling plus the relationship bonding the two.

It proves that the two, though distinct and separate, are interdependent.

More and more, project planners and schedulers are under scrutiny by their more hands-on project team members. Much to their despair and consternation; construction managers, supervisors, superintendents, engineers and other stakeholders brush them aside, discounting their importance whenever the chance presents itself.

Such attitudes have no place to a savvy and up to snap project professional while a less prepared peer will cringe, and melt, terrified to make the proper response.

It is also an excellent opportunity to draw the attention of the readers to the author's philosophy that all planning and scheduling process are risk-based.

Available in PM Solution Pro (https://pmsolutionpro.com), Amazon.com, Chapters, Indigo, and various international outlets and bookstores in paperback and e-book.

"How to Create a Good Quality P50 Risk-based Baseline Schedule"

ISBN 978-0-9947608-1-4

Project Managers know what they want. They want achievable schedule that delivers timely execution. For one reason or another, many have tried, and many have failed.

The most pressing root cause however is quite simple. One of the major reasons of schedule overrun is varying certainties of each schedule activity. The greater the difference between driving predecessor and driven successor activities, the greater the impact to the end date. This problem is underscored in this book. The author recommends the creation of a P50 solution using the more common management tools available OPRA and P6.

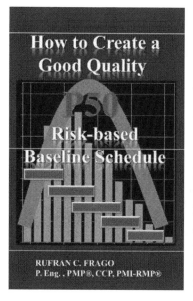

With cost and time burdens greater than ever before in a project set up, projects must be creative and find workable ways to increase probability of successfully completing target dates and durations.

Even schedules put together based on years of know-how, years of experience, and best practice cannot always accurately predict the future.

There is no absolute guarantee to the behavior of a present-day projects. Schedule certainty is in doubt every time a project ignores schedule quality. In view of this, a probability estimate that includes schedule quality, and align certainty in the equation deserves praise. Quantified schedule risks without respect for quality compounds errors over time to give management a false assessment of the outcome.

Creating a Good Quality P50 Risk-based Baseline Schedule is a relatively new approach to developing project schedule execution baseline. Adopting the approach needs added understanding of the rationale surrounding its use. The rationale traces the influence quality, identified risk, and estimate uncertainty on the schedule. An adjustment in insight is needed for the reader to appreciate how varying activity certainties adversely affects the time objectives. The book touches on schedule alignment, integration, risk, achievability and the consequence of ignoring them.

The step-by-step instructions on how to develop a P50 Risk-based Baseline Schedule is detailed in this book. The concept is clear, so why not try it in your next project and let us know what happened. The book is for risk and project management practitioners who want to try something new and reasonable. Read this short-illustrated book, find out, and decide for yourself.

Available in PM Solution Pro (https://pmsolutionpro.com), Amazon.com, Chapters, Indigo, and various international outlets and bookstores in paperback and e-book.

Coming Soon!

RISK, What are you?

(The Risk Management Poem)

ISBN: 978-0-9947608-4-5 (Canada)

Text copyright © March 2019 Rufran C. Frago
CIPO Registration No. 1157695
All Rights Reserved

39525497R00157

Made in the USA
Middletown, DE
20 March 2019